One Common Bond

Daily Affirmations for Men Struggling with Loneliness,

Sense of Purpose, and Belonging

Copyright © 2026 Johnny King

All rights reserved.

ISBN-13: 979-8-9944449-0-0

Dedication

To my kids; Ayven, Logan, Brynn, and Holden
I sought out support so that I would be better able to support you.

To the most supportive group of guys I have ever met; Jeff, Brian, and Matt;
#HOMETEAM #ONEBOAT

Preface

The meaning behind One Common Bond
\>\>\>\>\>\>\>

I began writing this book in 2024. It was one of the hardest times in my life. Two of my closest caregivers growing up, my father and maternal grandmother, had passed away within a year of each other. On top of that, I had been separated from my wife for nearly a year, and the month before I would start writing this, she informed me that she wanted a divorce. Suffice to say, things were not going my way.

But one of the things that kept me going was that I had recently stared attending a 10-week course on Self-Worth for Men. It was just me and three other guys, learning how to see the value in ourselves.

It was apparent pretty quickly that our backgrounds were very different from one another, but we shared <u>one common bond</u>;

<u>We were all searching for the value within ourselves</u>.

At the age of 38, I forged a bond of friendship that I had never experienced with a group of men.

The ability to be real and vulnerable with these guys has transformed my life. We text and talk to each other nearly every day, and when someone has had a hard time or a victory, we feel safe to share with one another because we know that we have a group of guys who have our back.

That's ultimately what led me to write this book. There is an epidemic of loneliness impacting men all over the world and I have suffered from it firsthand. I want other men to find what I have found and experience the comfort of connection with other men who have your best interest at heart.

One Common Bond is a book of affirmations to encourage all men on their journey through life. It is my sincere hope that it will help you in times when you feel most alone, most afraid, most vulnerable, and maybe even during times when you don't want to be alive anymore. I get that. I have been there too.

After a month or two, you may feel like some of the affirmations seem familiar. This is on purpose. We don't release things like failure, guilt, and shame in one day. I've tried to space them out to where we come back to them often enough to help keep us mindful of them but no so often as to feel repetitive.

I end the affirmation every day with the same phrase:

We all struggle and suffer; You are not alone in it.

There is no shame in the struggle and suffering;

This is our one common bond.

You are enough; You are loved; You are worthy;

And you will never be alone.

I wrote these affirmations in a way that is most beneficial when you read them out loud. This helps your subconscious mind to internalize the ideas that are being presented. I strongly encourage you to say out loud to yourself the words "You are enough, you are loved, you are worthy and you will never be alone." Feel free to adapt these phrases in whatever way you feel benefits you most.

The cure to loneliness is community.

Before moving forward, please consider joining our free community at www.OneCommonBond.com

Or simply scan this QR code

If you are struggling with thoughts of suicide, please reach out to someone for help.

In the US, you can access the Suicide & Crisis Lifeline by dialing one of the following numbers:

988 ; 1-800-273-TALK ; 1-800-273-8255

Or you can text with the Lifeline chat at

www.suicidepreventionlifeline.org/chat

If you aren't in the United States, I encourage you to go to https://yourlifecounts.org/find-help/ to find help in your country/region.

January 1

Feeling isolated despite being around others
>>>>>>>

Today, I will remind myself that being surrounded by people doesn't mean I can't feel lonely. True connection isn't about the size of the crowd; it's about finding those who truly see and hear me. I will focus on seeking deeper bonds and remind myself that I deserve to be understood.

Sometimes, being around people can feel even lonelier. Like, everyone's there, but no one really sees you. I've felt that. The reality is that connection isn't about the number of people. It's about finding the *right* people.

So today, let's remind ourselves that we deserve to be seen, to be heard. Start small; reach out to someone who makes you feel understood or let someone know how you're really doing. Connection is possible, even in loneliness.

Remember that part having each other's backs means showing up for yourself as well.

We all struggle and suffer; You are not alone in it.

There is no shame in the struggle and suffering;

This is our one common bond.

You are enough; You are loved; You are worthy;

And you will never be alone.

January 2

Struggling to express emotions or vulnerabilities
\>>>>>>>

Today, I will take a small step toward expressing how I feel. Vulnerability is not a weakness. It's how we form real connections. By sharing a part of myself, I remind others and myself that emotions are meant to be felt, not hidden.

Opening up about how you feel can be hard. It's scary to think, 'What if they don't understand?' But being vulnerable doesn't mean you're weak. It means you're brave enough to share what's real.

So, start small. Maybe it's telling a friend what's been on your mind, or just writing it down for yourself. Every step toward openness is a step toward connection. And when we support each other in this, we remind ourselves that we're not alone.

We all struggle and suffer; You are not alone in it.

There is no shame in the struggle and suffering;

This is our one common bond.

You are enough; You are loved; You are worthy;

And you will never be alone.

January 3

Dealing with societal expectations of stoicism
\>\>\>\>\>\>\>

Today, I remind myself that strength isn't about hiding how I feel; it's about being honest with myself. I refuse to let outdated expectations hold me back. I will redefine what strength looks like for me.

How many times have you heard, 'Man up'? Like showing emotions somehow makes you weak. But I've learned that real strength isn't about hiding what you feel. It's about being honest with yourself and others.

So today, let's push back against unhealthy, outdated expectations. Let's show each other that being open and real is what makes us strong. Together, we can redefine what strength looks like.

We all struggle and suffer; You are not alone in it.

There is no shame in the struggle and suffering;

This is our one common bond.

You are enough; You are loved; You are worthy;

And you will never be alone.

January 4

Coping with grief or loss
>>>>>>>

Today, I honor the memory of what I've lost. Grief is not something I need to 'fix.' It's something I carry with me as a reminder of love. I will allow myself to feel without judgment and remind myself that I am not alone in this.

Grief is one of those things that never really leaves. It's heavy, and it can hit you out of nowhere. But grief isn't a weakness. It's love that doesn't have a place to go.

If you're grieving today, know that it's okay to feel whatever you're feeling. Honor that love. And remember, you don't have to carry it alone. Together, we can share the weight of grief.

We all struggle and suffer; You are not alone in it.

There is no shame in the struggle and suffering;

This is our one common bond.

You are enough; You are loved; You are worthy; And you will never be alone.

January 5

Fear of rejection when reaching out to others
>>>>>>>

Today, I will take the risk to reach out. I remind myself that rejection doesn't define my worth. It's simply a part of trying. I am worthy of connection, and I will give myself permission to seek it.

Reaching out can feel terrifying, right? That fear of, 'What if they don't care? What if they say no?' But rejection doesn't mean you're unworthy. It just means that connection takes time and courage.

Today, let's take that first step. Whether it's sending a message, asking for help, or just saying hi, it's worth the risk. Because connection is possible, and you're not alone in this.

We all struggle and suffer; You are not alone in it.

There is no shame in the struggle and suffering;

This is our one common bond.

You are enough; You are loved; You are worthy;

And you will never be alone.

January 6

Struggling with self-worth and self-esteem
>>>>>>>

Today, I will remind myself that my worth isn't tied to what I accomplish or how others see me. I am valuable just as I am, and I will treat myself with the respect and kindness I deserve.

It's easy to feel like your worth depends on what you achieve, or how others see you. But that's not the truth. Your worth isn't something you have to earn; it's something you already have.

So today, let's remind ourselves to treat ourselves with kindness. Take a moment to appreciate who you are, not what you've done. And if it feels hard, just know you're not alone in this.

We all struggle and suffer; You are not alone in it.

There is no shame in the struggle and suffering;

This is our one common bond.

You are enough; You are loved; You are worthy;

And you will never be alone.

January 7

Coping with the end of a relationship
>>>>>>>

Today, I will allow myself to grieve what I've lost, while reminding myself that this loss does not define my future. I am worthy of love and connection, and I will take this time to rebuild with compassion for myself.

The end of a relationship can feel like the end of everything, can't it? Like you've lost a part of yourself. But here's what I want to remind you: this loss doesn't define you. It's okay to grieve, to feel the hurt.

But it's also okay to start rebuilding, little by little. You're still worthy of love, of connection, of happiness. And even if it feels like you're alone right now, you're not. We're in this together.

We all struggle and suffer; You are not alone in it.

There is no shame in the struggle and suffering;

This is our one common bond.

You are enough; You are loved; You are worthy;

And you will never be alone.

January 8

Feeling invisible or unimportant
>>>>>>>

Today, I remind myself that my value is not determined by how others see me. I matter, even if I feel unseen. I will take steps to remind myself of my worth and seek spaces where I am valued.

Have you ever felt invisible, like you could disappear and no one would notice? It's a tough feeling; like you don't matter. But I want you to hear this: you do matter.

Your worth isn't determined by how much attention you get or who sees you. You matter because of who you are, not how others make you feel.

Let's remind each other to find spaces where we're valued and to value ourselves even when it's hard. You're not invisible here.

We all struggle and suffer; You are not alone in it.

There is no shame in the struggle and suffering;

This is our one common bond.

You are enough; You are loved; You are worthy;

And you will never be alone.

January 9

Missing a sense of belonging or community
>>>>>>>

Today, I will take one small step to build or find a sense of belonging. I deserve to feel connected, and I will seek out people or places that value and support me.

Belonging is something we all crave, but it's hard when you feel like you don't fit anywhere. Maybe you've tried and it hasn't worked, or maybe you don't even know where to start.

But belonging isn't about fitting in everywhere. It's about finding the people and places where you can be yourself.

Take one small step today. Maybe it's joining a group, reaching out to someone, or just reminding yourself that you're worthy of connection. Together, we can create spaces where we all belong.

We all struggle and suffer; You are not alone in it.

There is no shame in the struggle and suffering;

This is our one common bond.

You are enough; You are loved; You are worthy;

And you will never be alone.

January 10

Struggling to forgive yourself for past mistakes
>>>>>>>

Today, I choose to let go of the guilt I've been carrying. My mistakes do not define me, and I will allow myself to grow and move forward. I deserve forgiveness, especially from myself.

Mistakes don't mean you're broken. They mean you tried, and you're still here, still growing.

If guilt is heavy today, remind yourself that every step forward, no matter how small, is proof that you are healing. Let's keep going.

We all struggle and suffer; You are not alone in it.

There is no shame in the struggle and suffering;

This is our one common bond.

You are enough; You are loved; You are worthy;

And you will never be alone.

January 11

Struggling with body image or physical health concerns
>>>>>>>

Today, I will treat my body with kindness. My worth is not defined by how I look, and I will focus on taking care of myself in ways that feel good and empowering.

Body image is something a lot of us struggle with, even if we don't talk about it. Maybe you feel like you don't look how you're 'supposed' to, or you're not as strong or healthy as you want to be.

Here is what matters: your worth isn't defined by your appearance. Your body is yours. It's carried you through life, through every challenge and every triumph.

So today, let's focus on treating our bodies with kindness. Take a step toward health, not perfection. And remind yourself that you're valuable just as you are.

We all struggle and suffer; You are not alone in it.

There is no shame in the struggle and suffering;

This is our one common bond.

You are enough; You are loved; You are worthy;

And you will never be alone.

January 12

Difficulty opening up about mental health struggles
>>>>>>>

Today, I remind myself that talking about mental health is not a weakness; it's a strength. I will take one step toward sharing my struggles, knowing that I deserve support and understanding.

Talking about mental health can feel like the hardest thing in the world. Maybe you've been told to 'suck it up' or 'deal with it on your own.' Let's be real; asking for help isn't weak. It's brave.

Today, let's remind ourselves that it's okay to struggle. And it's okay to talk about it. Start small by sharing a little with someone you trust, or even just write it down for yourself.

When we open up, we remind ourselves and others of our common bond.

We all struggle and suffer; You are not alone in it.

There is no shame in the struggle and suffering;

This is our one common bond.

You are enough; You are loved; You are worthy;

And you will never be alone.

January 13

Feeling disconnected from personal values or faith
>>>>>>>

Today, I will reconnect with what matters most to me. Whether it's my values, my faith, or my sense of purpose, I will take time to reflect and realign with what brings me meaning.

Have you ever felt like you've lost touch with what really matters to you? Like the things that used to give you meaning just don't feel the same? It's a hard place to be.

But here's the thing: it's okay to take time to reconnect. Whether it's through quiet reflection, talking to someone, or just trying to be present in the moment, you can find your way back to what matters most.

Let's remind each other to take that time, to realign with what brings us peace and purpose.

We all struggle and suffer; You are not alone in it.

There is no shame in the struggle and suffering;

This is our one common bond.

You are enough; You are loved; You are worthy;

And you will never be alone.

January 14

Struggling with burnout or exhaustion without support
>>>>>>>

Today, I will give myself permission to rest. Rest is not laziness; It's how I regain strength. I deserve to take care of myself, and I will remind myself that asking for support is a sign of courage, not weakness.

Burnout feels like you're running on empty, doesn't it? Like no matter how hard you try, there's nothing left to give. But here's what I've learned: Rest isn't a luxury. It's a necessity.

Today, let's give ourselves permission to slow down, to breathe, to take a break. And let's remind each other that it's okay to ask for help when we need it. Because rest isn't something you have to earn; it's something you deserve.

You don't have to carry it all alone.

We all struggle and suffer; You are not alone in it.

There is no shame in the struggle and suffering;

This is our one common bond.

You are enough; You are loved; You are worthy;

And you will never be alone.

January 15

Feeling unappreciated or taken for granted
>>>>>>>

Today, I remind myself that my worth is not tied to how others recognize me. I am valuable, even if it goes unnoticed. I will seek spaces and people who see and appreciate me for who I am.

Feeling unappreciated can be so disheartening, can't it? Like you're giving so much, but no one even notices. But here's what I want to remind you: your worth doesn't depend on anyone else's recognition.

You are valuable, just as you are. And while it's okay to want to feel seen, don't forget to see yourself too. Let's support each other in finding spaces where we're truly appreciated. Because when we remind each other of our value, we prove that we're not alone.

We all struggle and suffer; You are not alone in it.

There is no shame in the struggle and suffering;

This is our one common bond.

You are enough; You are loved; You are worthy;

And you will never be alone.

January 16

Coping with family estrangement or conflict
>>>>>>>

Today, I acknowledge that family relationships can be difficult, and I will give myself permission to protect my peace. I will focus on building connections that bring positivity and healing into my life.

Family conflict can be one of the hardest things to deal with, especially when you feel like you're caught in the middle or pushed away. But here's the thing: you're allowed to protect your peace.

You're allowed to set boundaries, to focus on relationships that bring you love and understanding. And if family has let you down, know this: you can still create a family through the connections you build.

You don't have to face this pain alone. Let's support each other in finding the connections that heal us.

We all struggle and suffer; You are not alone in it.

There is no shame in the struggle and suffering;

This is our one common bond.

You are enough; You are loved; You are worthy;

And you will never be alone.

January 17

Struggling with financial stress without someone to talk to
>>>>>>>

Today, I will remind myself that my worth is not tied to my financial situation. I will take one small step toward addressing my stress and remind myself that seeking help is a strength, not a weakness.

Financial stress can feel so isolating. It's hard to talk about, and even harder to ask for help. The truth you need to believe is that your value as a person isn't tied to your bank account.

Take one small step today. Whether it's creating a plan, reaching out for advice, or just reminding yourself that you're more than your circumstances. We all face challenges like this, and you're not alone in figuring it out.

We all struggle and suffer; You are not alone in it.

There is no shame in the struggle and suffering;

This is our one common bond.

You are enough; You are loved; You are worthy;

And you will never be alone.

January 18

Fear of being a burden to others
>>>>>>>

Today, I will remind myself that needing help does not make me a burden. Asking for support is how we grow closer to others. I deserve to be supported, just as I support those around me.

Do you ever feel like asking for help makes you a burden? Like your struggles are too much for anyone else to handle? I've felt that too. I learned the hard way that needing help doesn't make you a burden. It makes you human.

When we let others support us, we create deeper connections. We show them that it's okay to lean on each other. So today, let's remind ourselves that we're not too much.

We all struggle and suffer; You are not alone in it.

There is no shame in the struggle and suffering;

This is our one common bond.

You are enough; You are loved; You are worthy;

And you will never be alone.

January 19

Coping with the gap between how life is and how it was envisioned
>>>>>>>

Today, I accept that my path may not look the way I imagined, but it still holds value. I will focus on what I can create moving forward, reminding myself that growth happens even in unexpected places.

Life doesn't always turn out the way we imagined, does it? Sometimes, the gap between where we are and where we thought we'd be feels overwhelming. But here's what I've learned: even when life doesn't follow the plan, it can still be meaningful.

Take a moment to look at what you've overcome, what you've built along the way. It's okay to grieve the vision you had, but don't forget to embrace the possibilities still ahead. And remember; you're not walking this road alone.

We all struggle and suffer; You are not alone in it.

There is no shame in the struggle and suffering;

This is our one common bond.

You are enough; You are loved; You are worthy;

And you will never be alone.

January 20

Struggling to maintain work-life balance
>>>>>>>

Today, I will remind myself that my worth is not tied to how much I accomplish. I will prioritize rest and connection, knowing that balance is key to a meaningful life.

Work can take over so easily, can't it? Like there's always one more thing to do, one more goal to reach. But here's what I want you to remember: your worth isn't tied to how much you get done.

Today, let's take a step back. Let's focus on finding balance: Making time for rest, for connection, for the things that make life meaningful. Work is important, but it's not everything. And you don't have to navigate this balance alone.

We all struggle and suffer; You are not alone in it.

There is no shame in the struggle and suffering;

This is our one common bond.

You are enough; You are loved; You are worthy;

And you will never be alone.

January 21

Dealing with judgment or criticism for showing emotions
>>>>>>>

Today, I remind myself that showing emotions is a sign of strength, not weakness. I will honor how I feel and refuse to let the judgment of others diminish my humanity

Have you ever been told to 'toughen up' when you're just trying to be real about how you feel? It's frustrating, isn't it? Like showing emotions makes you less of a man.

But let me tell you this; being honest about how you feel isn't weakness. It's strength. It's courage. It's what makes you human.

So today, let's remind ourselves to honor our emotions, no matter what anyone says. And let's support each other in creating a world where it's okay to feel. Because you're not alone in this.

We all struggle and suffer; You are not alone in it.

There is no shame in the struggle and suffering;

This is our one common bond.

You are enough; You are loved; You are worthy;

And you will never be alone.

January 22

Fear of vulnerability leading to emotional distance
>>>>>>>

Today, I will remind myself that vulnerability is the bridge to connection. I will take small steps to open up, knowing that true relationships are built on trust and honesty.

Sometimes, being vulnerable feels like taking a huge risk. It's scary to think, 'What if I open up and get hurt?' So instead, we put up walls. But those walls don't protect us; they isolate us.

Vulnerability is how we create connection. It's how we remind ourselves and others that we're human. Start small by sharing a little bit of what you're feeling with someone you trust.

It's not easy, but it's worth it. Because when we open up, we find connection.

We all struggle and suffer; You are not alone in it.

There is no shame in the struggle and suffering;

This is our one common bond.

You are enough; You are loved; You are worthy;

And you will never be alone.

January 23

Struggling to rebuild trust after being hurt
>>>>>>>

Today, I will take steps to rebuild trust. Not only in others but in myself. I will remind myself that trust is earned over time, and I deserve relationships where trust and respect are mutual.

Trust can be so hard to rebuild after you've been hurt. It's tempting to close yourself off, to think, 'I'll never let this happen again.' But here's what I've learned: while it's okay to protect yourself, it's also okay to let people in slowly.

Rebuilding trust takes time; both in others and in yourself. It's a process, but you're not alone in it. Let's remind each other that trust is worth rebuilding, one step at a time.

We all struggle and suffer; You are not alone in it.

There is no shame in the struggle and suffering;

This is our one common bond.

You are enough; You are loved; You are worthy;

And you will never be alone.

January 24

Dealing with toxic masculinity in social circles
>>>>>>>

Today, I will reject toxic behaviors that don't serve me or others. I will define what being a man means to me, and I will seek relationships that encourage kindness, respect, and authenticity.

Have you ever felt pressure to act a certain way just because you're a guy? To fit into a mold that doesn't really feel like you? That's toxic masculinity, and it doesn't have to define us.

Being a man isn't about being tough or stoic. It's about being authentic. It's about respect, kindness, and being real. Let's support each other in breaking free from those expectations.

Together, we can create spaces where being yourself feels safe.

We all struggle and suffer; You are not alone in it.

There is no shame in the struggle and suffering;

This is our one common bond.

You are enough; You are loved; You are worthy;

And you will never be alone.

January 25

Feeling ashamed for struggling emotionally or mentally
\>>>>>>>

Today, I will remind myself that struggling doesn't make me weak; it makes me human. I will take one small step toward acknowledging and addressing my feelings with compassion.

Have you ever felt ashamed for struggling? Like you should have it all together? I've been there. But here's what I've learned: struggling doesn't make you weak. It makes you human.

It's okay to admit when you're not okay. It's okay to take the time you need to heal. Let's remind each other that there's no shame in struggling. You don't have to face this alone.

We all struggle and suffer; You are not alone in it.

There is no shame in the struggle and suffering;

This is our one common bond.

You are enough; You are loved; You are worthy;

And you will never be alone.

January 26

Coping with addiction or harmful habits in isolation
>>>>>>>

Today, I remind myself that asking for help is a step toward healing. I deserve support, and I will take one small step to address the habits that no longer serve me.

Dealing with addiction or harmful habits can feel incredibly isolating. It's easy to think, 'I should be able to fix this on my own.' But healing doesn't happen in isolation.

It's okay to ask for help. It's okay to reach out to someone who can support you. One small step today can lead to big changes tomorrow. Let's remind each other that recovery is possible.

We all struggle and suffer; You are not alone in it.

There is no shame in the struggle and suffering;

This is our one common bond.

You are enough; You are loved; You are worthy;

And you will never be alone.

January 27

Struggling with comparison to others' lives or achievements
>>>>>>>

Today, I will focus on my own path. Comparing myself to others only distracts me from my unique journey. I will celebrate my progress and remind myself that my worth is not defined by comparison.

Have you ever scrolled through social media and thought, 'Everyone else has it all together, why don't I?' It's easy to compare yourself to others, but here's the thing: their journey isn't yours.

Your worth isn't defined by what someone else is doing. You're on your own path, and that path is valid. Let's remind each other to focus on progress, not comparison. You're not alone in this.

We all struggle and suffer; You are not alone in it.

There is no shame in the struggle and suffering;

This is our one common bond.

You are enough; You are loved; You are worthy;

And you will never be alone.

January 28

Struggling to make decisions without guidance or support
\>\>\>\>\>\>\>

Today, I remind myself that I am capable of making decisions, even when they feel difficult. I will trust my instincts and seek support when I need it, knowing that I don't have to face this alone.

Making decisions can feel overwhelming, especially when you feel like you're on your own. But here's what I want you to remember: you're capable. You've made it this far, and you can keep going.

It's okay to trust yourself. And it's okay to ask for advice when you need it. You don't have to figure everything out alone. Let's remind each other that support is always there.

We all struggle and suffer; You are not alone in it.

There is no shame in the struggle and suffering;

This is our one common bond.

You are enough; You are loved; You are worthy;

And you will never be alone.

January 29

Coping with unemployment or career instability
>>>>>>>

Today, I will remind myself that my value is not tied to my job title or income. I am more than my work, and I will take steps to create stability and purpose in my own time.

Unemployment or career instability can make you feel like you've lost a part of yourself. But your worth isn't tied to your job title or paycheck.

You're more than your work. Take things one step at a time, and remember that it's okay to ask for support along the way. Together, we can remind each other of our value, no matter where we are in life.

We all struggle and suffer; You are not alone in it.

There is no shame in the struggle and suffering;

This is our one common bond.

You are enough; You are loved; You are worthy;

And you will never be alone.

January 30

Coping with grief during special occasions
>>>>>>>

Today, I will allow myself to feel whatever I need to feel. Special occasions can bring both joy and pain, and that's okay. I will honor my grief while staying open to moments of connection and peace.

Special occasions can be bittersweet when you're grieving. It's okay to miss them, to wish they were still here. But it's also okay to find moments of peace and connection, even in the pain.

Let's remind each other that grief and joy can coexist. You don't have to face these moments alone.

We all struggle and suffer; You are not alone in it.

There is no shame in the struggle and suffering;

This is our one common bond.

You are enough; You are loved; You are worthy;

And you will never be alone.

January 31

Finding strength in gratitude
>>>>>>>

Today, I will focus on the things I am grateful for. Gratitude reminds me of the good in my life and gives me strength to keep moving forward.

Gratitude has a way of shifting your perspective, doesn't it? It reminds you of what's good, even when life feels heavy.

Take a moment today to think about one thing you're grateful for. It can be big or small. Let's remind each other that gratitude brings strength.

We all struggle and suffer; You are not alone in it.

There is no shame in the struggle and suffering;

This is our one common bond.

You are enough; You are loved; You are worthy;

And you will never be alone.

February 1

Struggling to connect with others after a major life change
>>>>>>>

Today, I remind myself that it's okay to feel disconnected after a big change. Building new connections takes time, and I will take small steps toward finding my people.

Life changes can be tough, can't they? Whether it's moving, a new job, or something unexpected, it can feel like the connections you had don't fit anymore. But here's what I want you to remember: finding your people takes time.

Take it one step at a time. Whether it's reaching out, joining something new, or just giving yourself grace to adjust. You're not alone in figuring this out.

We all struggle and suffer; You are not alone in it.

There is no shame in the struggle and suffering;

This is our one common bond.

You are enough; You are loved; You are worthy;

And you will never be alone.

February 2

Feeling stuck in repetitive or unfulfilling routines
\>>>>>>>

Today, I remind myself that it's okay to feel disconnected after a big change. Building new connections takes time, and I will take small steps toward finding my people.

Today, I remind myself that I am not trapped by my routines. I can make small changes to bring joy and meaning into my day, even in unexpected places.

Does life ever feel like you're just going through the motions? Same routine, day after day? It's easy to feel stuck, but here's the thing: you're not trapped.

Even small changes; a walk outside, trying something new, or reaching out to someone can make a difference. Let's remind each other that it's okay to seek joy, even in the smallest ways. You're not stuck, and you're not alone.

We all struggle and suffer; You are not alone in it.

There is no shame in the struggle and suffering;

This is our one common bond.

You are enough; You are loved; You are worthy;

And you will never be alone.

February 3

Struggling with social anxiety or fear of judgment
>>>>>>>

Today, I will remind myself that I am enough just as I am. I will take one small step to engage with others, knowing that I don't have to be perfect to connect.

Social anxiety can feel overwhelming, like every word you say or step you take is being judged. But here's what I want to remind you: most people aren't judging. They're just as focused on their own stuff as you are.

Take one small step today by saying hi, joining a conversation, or just being present. Connection doesn't have to be perfect to be meaningful. Let's remind each other that we're enough, just as we are.

We all struggle and suffer; You are not alone in it.

There is no shame in the struggle and suffering;

This is our one common bond.

You are enough; You are loved; You are worthy;

And you will never be alone.

February 4

Struggling to find purpose or direction in life
>>>>>>>

Today, I remind myself that purpose doesn't have to be big or perfect. I will focus on small actions that bring meaning to my day, knowing that my path will unfold over time.

Do you ever feel like you're searching for something, but you're not even sure what it is? Like you're stuck waiting for a sense of purpose to show up? I've been there.

But purpose doesn't have to be huge or clear right away. It can start with small things like helping someone, creating something, or just taking care of yourself.

Let's remind each other that our paths will unfold in their own time. Purpose grows from small, meaningful steps.

We all struggle and suffer; You are not alone in it.

There is no shame in the struggle and suffering;

This is our one common bond.

You are enough; You are loved; You are worthy;

And you will never be alone.

February 5

Fear of being abandoned or forgotten
>>>>>>>

Today, I remind myself that I am not defined by others leaving. I will focus on building relationships based on mutual care and trust, knowing that I am worthy of connection.

Do you ever worry that the people in your life might leave, or that you might be forgotten? That fear is hard to carry, but recognize this: the right people won't abandon you.

Focus on building relationships where you feel valued and supported. And remind yourself that you're worthy of connection, no matter what. You're not alone in this.

We all struggle and suffer; You are not alone in it.

There is no shame in the struggle and suffering;

This is our one common bond.

You are enough; You are loved; You are worthy;

And you will never be alone.

February 6

Finding peace in imperfection
>>>>>>>

Today, I will remind myself that things don't have to be perfect to be meaningful. I will focus on the beauty in what is, not what 'should' be.

Do you ever feel like everything has to be perfect to count? Like the imperfections ruin the moment? Just remember that life isn't perfect, and it doesn't have to be.

Take a moment today to find beauty in something imperfect around you. Let's remind each other that what's real is what matters.

We all struggle and suffer; You are not alone in it.

There is no shame in the struggle and suffering;

This is our one common bond.

You are enough; You are loved; You are worthy;

And you will never be alone.

February 7

Building moments of connection
>>>>>>>

Today, I will focus on creating moments of connection. I will remind myself that even brief, meaningful interactions bring joy and belonging.

Connection doesn't have to be complicated. A quick check-in, a genuine smile, or a kind word can remind someone they're cared for.

Take a moment today to create one small moment of connection with someone. Let's remind each other that connection is everywhere if we look for it.

We all struggle and suffer; You are not alone in it.

There is no shame in the struggle and suffering;

This is our one common bond.

You are enough; You are loved; You are worthy;

And you will never be alone.

February 8

Struggling with shame from past mistakes
>>>>>>>

Today, I will choose compassion over guilt. My past mistakes do not define me, and I will allow myself the grace to grow and move forward.

Letting go of past mistakes can be so hard, can't it? It's easy to replay them in your mind, feeling like they define you. But here's the thing: they don't.

Your mistakes don't make you unworthy. Making mistakes is just part of being human. Today, let's take one small step toward self-forgiveness. Growth starts with compassion, and you don't have to do it alone.

We all struggle and suffer; You are not alone in it.

There is no shame in the struggle and suffering;

This is our one common bond.

You are enough; You are loved; You are worthy;

And you will never be alone.

February 9

Difficulty finding a creative or emotional outlet
>>>>>>>

Today, I will explore new ways to express myself. Creativity doesn't have to be perfect. It's about connection and release. I will allow myself to try, knowing there is no wrong way to create.

Sometimes, it feels like there's no way to let out what's inside; no outlet for the emotions or ideas building up. But creativity isn't about being perfect. It's about expressing yourself, however that looks.

Maybe it's writing, drawing, playing music, or just talking it out with someone you trust. Whatever you try, it's valid. Let's remind each other that there's no wrong way to create. You don't have to keep it all inside.

We all struggle and suffer; You are not alone in it.

There is no shame in the struggle and suffering;

This is our one common bond.

You are enough; You are loved; You are worthy;

And you will never be alone.

February 10

Feeling like life lacks joy or excitement
>>>>>>>

Today, I will remind myself that joy can be found in small moments. I will look for opportunities to bring light into my day, no matter how simple they seem.

Do you ever feel like life's just... dull? Like there's no joy or excitement anymore? It's a heavy feeling. But joy doesn't have to come from big moments.

It's in the small things like kind word, a favorite song, the way sunlight feels on your face. Let's encourage each other to notice those little moments and let them bring us back to life. You're not alone in finding joy again.

We all struggle and suffer; You are not alone in it.

There is no shame in the struggle and suffering;

This is our one common bond.

You are enough; You are loved; You are worthy;

And you will never be alone.

February 11

Coping with unresolved childhood trauma
>>>>>>>

Today, I remind myself that healing is a journey, not a destination. I will take steps to address the pain I've carried, knowing I am worthy of peace and understanding.

Trauma from childhood is something we all carry in one way or another. It can shape how we see ourselves and the world, often without us realizing it. But here's what I want to remind you: healing is possible.

It's not about forgetting or ignoring. It's about understanding and moving forward. Take one step today, whether it's journaling, talking to someone, or just acknowledging the pain. You don't have to face it alone.

We all struggle and suffer; You are not alone in it.

There is no shame in the struggle and suffering;

This is our one common bond.

You are enough; You are loved; You are worthy;

And you will never be alone.

February 12

Dealing with chronic illness or disability alone
>>>>>>>

Today, I will remind myself that my challenges do not define my worth. I will seek support where I can and show myself the kindness I deserve.

Living with chronic illness or disability can feel isolating, like no one really understands what you're going through. But here's the thing: your challenges don't define your value.

You are so much more than what you're facing. It's okay to seek support, to ask for understanding, and to give yourself grace. Let's remind each other that even in the hardest moments, we're not alone.

We all struggle and suffer; You are not alone in it.

There is no shame in the struggle and suffering;

This is our one common bond.

You are enough; You are loved; You are worthy;

And you will never be alone.

February 13

Struggling with self-worth after a breakup
>>>>>>>

Today, I remind myself that a breakup does not determine my value. I will use this time to focus on my growth and healing, knowing I am worthy of love and connection.

Breakups can feel like they take a piece of you, can't they? Like they leave you questioning your worth. But here's what I want you to remember: your value isn't defined by a relationship.

This is a time to focus on you; to heal, to grow, and to remind yourself that you're worthy of love, both from others and yourself. Let's support each other in these moments. You're not alone in this.

We all struggle and suffer; You are not alone in it.

There is no shame in the struggle and suffering;

This is our one common bond.

You are enough; You are loved; You are worthy;

And you will never be alone.

February 14

Coping with loneliness on Valentine's Day
\>>>>>>>

Today, I will celebrate the love I give and receive in all its forms. Valentine's Day is a reminder that love is not limited to romance; it's found in friendships, family, and the way I care for myself.

Valentine's Day can be tough when you're feeling lonely. It's easy to feel like it's a reminder of what you don't have. But here's what I want you to remember: love isn't just about romance.

It's in the friendships you've built, the family you cherish, and the care you show yourself. Take today to celebrate those forms of love, because they matter just as much.

We all struggle and suffer; You are not alone in it.

There is no shame in the struggle and suffering;

This is our one common bond.

You are enough; You are loved; You are worthy;

And you will never be alone.

February 15

Struggling with forgiveness for others
>>>>>>>

Today, I remind myself that forgiveness is for my peace, not theirs. I will take steps to let go of resentment, freeing myself from the weight of anger.

Forgiveness can be one of the hardest things to do, can't it? Especially when someone's hurt you deeply. But here's what I've learned: forgiveness isn't about letting them off the hook. It's about freeing yourself.

Take one step today, even if it's just acknowledging the anger and choosing to let a little bit of it go. Let's remind each other that forgiveness is a gift we give ourselves.

We all struggle and suffer; You are not alone in it.

There is no shame in the struggle and suffering;

This is our one common bond.

You are enough; You are loved; You are worthy;

And you will never be alone.

February 16

Coping with fear of aging
\>>>>>>>

Today, I remind myself that aging is a privilege, not a burden. I will focus on the growth and wisdom that come with time, embracing each stage of my journey.

Aging can feel scary, especially when you think about what it means for your relationships, your health, or your goals. But here's what I want you to remember: aging is a privilege.

Every year you've lived is a testament to your resilience, your growth, and your story. Let's embrace the wisdom that comes with time and support each other as we keep moving forward. You're not alone in this.

We all struggle and suffer; You are not alone in it.

There is no shame in the struggle and suffering;

This is our one common bond.

You are enough; You are loved; You are worthy;

And you will never be alone.

February 17

Struggling to rebuild after a setback
>>>>>>>

Today, I remind myself that setbacks are not the end of my story. I will take one step forward, knowing that every step brings me closer to where I want to be.

Setbacks can feel like starting over, can't they? Like all the progress you've made is gone. But here's the truth: a setback isn't the end. It's just a chapter in your story.

Take one step today, no matter how small, and remind yourself that rebuilding is still progress. We're in this together, and you're not alone in starting again.

We all struggle and suffer; You are not alone in it.

There is no shame in the struggle and suffering;

This is our one common bond.

You are enough; You are loved; You are worthy;

And you will never be alone.

February 18

Feeling disconnected from others' experiences
\>>>>>>>

Today, I will remind myself that my journey is unique, and that's okay. I will seek connection through understanding and openness, knowing we all have something to share.

Toxic relationships can be so draining, can't they? They make you question yourself, your worth, and your place. But here's what I want you to remember: you deserve better.

You deserve relationships that uplift you, not tear you down. Setting boundaries or walking away isn't selfish. It's self-respect. Let's support each other in creating the connections we deserve.

We all struggle and suffer; You are not alone in it.

There is no shame in the struggle and suffering;

This is our one common bond.

You are enough; You are loved; You are worthy;

And you will never be alone.

February 19

Disconnection from others' experiences
>>>>>>>

Today, I will stay open to others, even when our paths are different. I will seek understanding over agreement, knowing that connection begins with curiosity.

It's easy to feel distant when you don't share someone's background or choices. But connection isn't about sameness. It's about listening.

Today, try asking instead of assuming. Share instead of shutting down. We grow closer when we stop trying to relate and start trying to understand.

We all struggle and suffer; You are not alone in it.

There is no shame in the struggle and suffering;

This is our one common bond.

You are enough; You are loved; You are worthy;

And you will never be alone.

February 20

Fear of failure holding you back
>>>>>>>

Today, I will remind myself that failure is a step on the path to growth. I will take one small action toward my goals, knowing that trying is always worth it.

Fear of failure can stop you in your tracks, can't it? It whispers, 'What if you're not good enough? What if you mess up?' But failure isn't the end. It's a step toward success.

Take one small action today, even if it feels scary. Trying is always worth it, and failure is just part of the journey. Let's support each other in taking that leap.

We all struggle and suffer; You are not alone in it.

There is no shame in the struggle and suffering;

This is our one common bond.

You are enough; You are loved; You are worthy;

And you will never be alone.

February 21

Coping with unresolved conflict
>>>>>>>

Today, I will remind myself that unresolved conflict does not have to control my peace. I will take steps to address or release the tension, knowing that I deserve clarity and closure.

Unresolved conflict can sit in the back of your mind, weighing you down even when you're not actively thinking about it. But you don't have to carry that weight forever.

Take one step today toward releasing that weight. Whether it's having the conversation, setting boundaries, or choosing to let it go. You deserve peace, and you don't have to face this alone.

We all struggle and suffer; You are not alone in it.

There is no shame in the struggle and suffering;

This is our one common bond.

You are enough; You are loved; You are worthy;

And you will never be alone.

February 22

Struggling with a sense of stagnation
>>>>>>>

Today, I will remind myself that progress doesn't have to be big to be meaningful. I will take small steps toward change, knowing that each step brings me closer to growth.

Do you ever feel stuck, like nothing's moving forward in your life? It's frustrating, isn't it? But here's what I want you to remember: even small steps count.

Progress doesn't have to be big or fast. It just has to move you forward. Take one small action today, and remind yourself that growth is still happening.

We all struggle and suffer; You are not alone in it.

There is no shame in the struggle and suffering;

This is our one common bond.

You are enough; You are loved; You are worthy;

And you will never be alone.

February 23

Struggling with guilt over past choices
>>>>>>>

Today, I will remind myself that guilt is a sign of growth, not a sentence to carry forever. I will use my past to learn and grow, knowing I am not defined by my mistakes.

Guilt can feel like a weight you can't put down, can't it? Like it's tied to you forever. But over time I've learned that guilt means that you care; it means you're growing.

Your past doesn't define you. What matters is what you choose to do now. Let's remind each other to use the past as a lesson, not a life sentence.

We all struggle and suffer; You are not alone in it.

There is no shame in the struggle and suffering;

This is our one common bond.

You are enough; You are loved; You are worthy;

And you will never be alone.

February 24

Struggling with burnout from caregiving
>>>>>>>

Today, I remind myself that caring for others doesn't mean neglecting myself. I will take moments to rest and recharge, knowing that I deserve care, too.

Being a caregiver is one of the hardest jobs, isn't it? You give so much of yourself to others that it feels like there's nothing left for you. But here's what I want you to remember: you deserve care, too.

It's okay to take breaks, to rest, and to ask for help. You can't pour from an empty cup. Let's remind each other that caring for ourselves makes us stronger for others.

We all struggle and suffer; You are not alone in it.

There is no shame in the struggle and suffering;

This is our one common bond.

You are enough; You are loved; You are worthy;

And you will never be alone.

February 25

Struggling with loneliness in a crowd
>>>>>>>

Today, I remind myself that feeling lonely doesn't mean I'm broken. I will seek meaningful connection, even if it starts with something small.

Being in a crowd can sometimes feel lonelier than being alone. Like everyone's connected, except you. But remember; feeling lonely doesn't mean you're broken.

Today I want you to make a small movement toward connection. Say hi to someone, start a conversation, or just let yourself be open to connection. Let's remind each other that we're all looking for the same thing.

We all struggle and suffer; You are not alone in it.

There is no shame in the struggle and suffering;

This is our one common bond.

You are enough; You are loved; You are worthy;

And you will never be alone.

February 26

Fear of asking for help
>>>>>>>

Today, I remind myself that asking for help is not a sign of failure, it's a step toward connection. I will reach out, knowing that I deserve support.

Asking for help can feel terrifying, like it's admitting you can't handle it all. But here's what I want you to remember: asking for help isn't weakness, it's courage.

Reach out today, even if it's just a small ask. Connection grows when we let others in. You don't have to do it all alone.

We all struggle and suffer; You are not alone in it.

There is no shame in the struggle and suffering;

This is our one common bond.

You are enough; You are loved; You are worthy;

And you will never be alone.

February 27

Struggling with societal pressure to have it all together
>>>>>>>

Today, I remind myself that no one has it all together, and that's okay. I will allow myself to be honest about where I am, knowing that growth takes time.

Society makes it seem like you're supposed to have everything figured out, doesn't it? Like if you don't, you're failing. But don't be fooled; no one has it all together.

It's okay to be a work in progress. Take things one step at a time, and remind yourself that growth happens in the mess. You're not alone in figuring it out.

We all struggle and suffer; You are not alone in it.

There is no shame in the struggle and suffering;

This is our one common bond.

You are enough; You are loved; You are worthy;

And you will never be alone.

February 28

Finding hope in uncertain times
\>>>>>>>

Today, I will focus on what I can control and let go of what I cannot. I will remind myself that hope can be found in small moments of progress and connection.

Uncertainty can feel overwhelming, can't it? Like the ground beneath you is always shifting. But here's what I want you to remember: even in uncertain times, there's hope.

Focus on what you can control: small actions, small moments of connection. Let's remind each other that we can build hope, even in the unknown.

We all struggle and suffer; You are not alone in it.

There is no shame in the struggle and suffering;

This is our one common bond.

You are enough; You are loved; You are worthy;

And you will never be alone.

February 29

Finding joy in giving to yourself
>>>>>>>

Today, I will remind myself that giving to myself is just as important as giving to others. I will take time to care for my own needs and well-being.

Sometimes it feels easier to take care of everyone else around you, but don't forget about yourself. Taking care of your own needs isn't selfish. It's how you recharge to give to others.

Take a moment today to do something for yourself, even if it's small. Let's remind each other that self-care is essential.

We all struggle and suffer; You are not alone in it.

There is no shame in the struggle and suffering;

This is our one common bond.

You are enough; You are loved; You are worthy;

And you will never be alone.

March 1

Embracing new beginnings
>>>>>>>

Today, I will remind myself that every day is a chance to start fresh. I will let go of the past and focus on the possibilities ahead, knowing that I am capable of creating change.

New beginnings can feel overwhelming, can't they? Like you're not sure where to start or if you're ready. But here's the thing: every day is a new chance.

It's okay to take small steps. Let today be the start of something better, no matter how small it seems. We're in this together.

We all struggle and suffer; You are not alone in it.

There is no shame in the struggle and suffering;

This is our one common bond.

You are enough; You are loved; You are worthy;

And you will never be alone.

March 2

Struggling with decision fatigue
>>>>>>>

Today, I will remind myself that it's okay to not have all the answers. I will take one decision at a time, trusting my instincts and seeking support when I need it.

Ever feel like the weight of all your decisions is just too much? Like you don't even know where to begin? I've been there.

But here's what I've learned: you don't have to figure it all out at once. Take one decision at a time. Trust yourself, and ask for help when you need it. You don't have to do this alone.

We all struggle and suffer; You are not alone in it.

There is no shame in the struggle and suffering;

This is our one common bond.

You are enough; You are loved; You are worthy;

And you will never be alone.

March 3

Fear of taking risks
>>>>>>>

Today, I remind myself that growth comes from stepping outside my comfort zone. I will take one small risk, knowing that every step forward is progress.

Taking risks can be terrifying, can't it? The fear of failing, of getting it wrong, can hold you back. But nothing changes if you stay in the same place.

Take one small step today, even if it feels scary. Every little risk brings you closer to growth. Let's remind each other that courage doesn't mean no fear. It means trying anyway.

We all struggle and suffer; You are not alone in it.

There is no shame in the struggle and suffering;

This is our one common bond.

You are enough; You are loved; You are worthy;

And you will never be alone.

March 4

Struggling with self-criticism
>>>>>>>

Today, I will be kind to myself. I will treat myself with the same compassion I offer to others, knowing that I am deserving of grace and understanding.

Do you ever find yourself being your own worst critic? Like you're harder on yourself than anyone else could ever be? I've felt that too.

But here's the thing: you deserve the same kindness you show others. Today, let's try to speak to ourselves with compassion. Let's remind each other that we're doing our best, and that's enough.

We all struggle and suffer; You are not alone in it.

There is no shame in the struggle and suffering;

This is our one common bond.

You are enough; You are loved; You are worthy;

And you will never be alone.

March 5

Struggling to stay motivated

\>>>>>>>

Today, I remind myself that progress doesn't have to be perfect to matter. I will celebrate small wins and keep moving forward, knowing that consistency is more important than speed.

Staying motivated can be hard, especially when progress feels slow. But hear this: progress doesn't have to be perfect to count. Even small steps matter. Celebrate those little wins, and remind yourself that consistency is the key. You're not alone in this journey.

We all struggle and suffer; You are not alone in it.

There is no shame in the struggle and suffering;

This is our one common bond.

You are enough; You are loved; You are worthy;

And you will never be alone.

March 6

Feeling like you don't belong

>>>>>>>

Today, I remind myself that I am worthy of belonging. I will seek out spaces and relationships that accept me for who I am, knowing that I deserve to feel connected.

Have you ever felt like you don't belong anywhere? Like no matter where you are, you're just not enough? It's a tough feeling, but here's what I want you to remember: you are worthy of belonging.

The right people and spaces are out there. They just take time to find. Let's encourage each other to keep looking, to keep reaching out. You're not alone in this search.

We all struggle and suffer; You are not alone in it.

There is no shame in the struggle and suffering;

This is our one common bond.

You are enough; You are loved; You are worthy;

And you will never be alone.

March 7

Rediscovering joy at your own pace

>>>>>>>

Today, I will remember that I am not late or behind; I'm right on time for my life. I will measure myself not by others' milestones, but by my own quiet victories.

Comparison steals joy, especially when we don't see the full picture.

So today, I'll pause. I'll acknowledge what I *have* done, what I *am* doing. Let's cheer for our progress, even if it looks different. Because our timelines are not a race—they're a reflection of our own beautiful path.

We all struggle and suffer; You are not alone in it.

There is no shame in the struggle and suffering;

This is our one common bond.

You are enough; You are loved; You are worthy;

And you will never be alone.

March 8

Shifting from regret to responsibility

>>>>>>>

Today, I will take ownership without shame. I will turn regret into responsibility, not to punish myself, but to grow. My past can be part of my healing.

It's not about pretending mistakes didn't happen. It's about choosing not to live inside them.

Let's remind ourselves and each other that accountability and self-love can exist side by side. Growth isn't perfect. But it's powerful.

We all struggle and suffer; You are not alone in it.

There is no shame in the struggle and suffering;

This is our one common bond.

You are enough; You are loved; You are worthy;

And you will never be alone.

March 9

Feeling overwhelmed by responsibilities

>>>>>>>

Today, I remind myself that I don't have to do it all at once. I will prioritize what matters most and allow myself the grace to rest when I need it.

Do you ever feel like your to-do list just keeps growing, no matter how much you do? It's overwhelming, isn't it? But here's what I want you to remember: you don't have to do it all at once. Prioritize what matters most. And don't forget to take breaks, because you deserve rest too. Let's remind each other that it's okay to go at your own pace.

We all struggle and suffer; You are not alone in it.

There is no shame in the struggle and suffering;

This is our one common bond.

You are enough; You are loved; You are worthy;

And you will never be alone.

March 10

Feeling disconnected from personal values

>>>>>>>

Today, I will take time to reflect on what matters most to me. I will align my actions with my values, knowing that I am capable of living a life that feels true to who I am.

Do you ever feel like you've lost touch with what really matters to you? Like you're just going through the motions? It's a tough place to be.
But here's the thing: it's never too late to realign.

Take a moment to reflect on your values, and find one small way to bring them back into focus. You're not alone in figuring this out.

We all struggle and suffer; You are not alone in it.

There is no shame in the struggle and suffering;

This is our one common bond.

You are enough; You are loved; You are worthy;

And you will never be alone.

# March 11

Struggling to find balance in life

>>>>>>>

Today, I remind myself that balance is not about perfection. It's about priorities. I will focus on what matters most and give myself grace for the rest.

Finding balance can feel impossible sometimes, can't it? Like there's always something pulling you in a different direction. But here's what I've learned: balance doesn't mean doing everything perfectly.
It's about focusing on what matters most and letting go of the rest.

Take a step today to prioritize what brings you peace. You're not alone in this.

We all struggle and suffer; You are not alone in it.

There is no shame in the struggle and suffering;

This is our one common bond.

You are enough; You are loved; You are worthy;

And you will never be alone.

March 12

Struggling with burnout at work

>>>>>>>

Today, I will remind myself that my worth is not tied to my productivity. I will take time to rest and recharge, knowing that I deserve balance in my work and life.

Burnout can creep up on you, can't it? One day you're handling everything, and the next it feels like you can't do anything. But we must believe that our worth isn't tied to how much we produce.

It's okay to take a step back, to rest, to recharge. You deserve balance in your work and life. Let's remind each other that it's okay to pause.

We all struggle and suffer; You are not alone in it.

There is no shame in the struggle and suffering;

This is our one common bond.

You are enough; You are loved; You are worthy;

And you will never be alone.

March 13

Coping with fear of rejection

>>>>>>>

Today, I remind myself that rejection is not a reflection of my worth. I will take the risk to reach out, knowing that connection is worth the effort.

Rejection can feel like the worst thing in the world, can't it? Like it's proof you're not good enough. But rejection isn't about your worth. It's just part of trying.

Take the risk today to reach out, to connect, to try again. Because connection is always worth it. Let's remind each other that we're not alone in taking chances.

We all struggle and suffer; You are not alone in it.

There is no shame in the struggle and suffering;

This is our one common bond.

You are enough; You are loved; You are worthy;

And you will never be alone.

March 14

Feeling stuck in a cycle of routine

>>>>>>>

Today, I remind myself that even small changes can bring new energy to my life. I will look for opportunities to break free from routine and try something new.

Do you ever feel like life is just the same thing over and over? Like you're stuck in a cycle you can't break? It's draining, isn't it? But here's the thing: even small changes can make a difference.

Try something new today. Take a different route, start a conversation, or explore a new hobby. Let's remind each other that life doesn't have to feel so repetitive.

We all struggle and suffer; You are not alone in it.

There is no shame in the struggle and suffering;

This is our one common bond.

You are enough; You are loved; You are worthy;

And you will never be alone.

March 15

Struggling with comparison to others' success

>>>>>>>

Today, I will remind myself that my path is unique. I will celebrate my progress, knowing that success looks different for everyone.

Do you ever look at someone else's life and think, 'Why am I not there yet?' It's so easy to compare, but remember that your path is your own.

Celebrate the steps you've taken, no matter how small they feel. Success doesn't have to look the same for everyone. Let's remind each other that we're all on our own journey.

We all struggle and suffer; You are not alone in it.

There is no shame in the struggle and suffering;

This is our one common bond.

You are enough; You are loved; You are worthy;

And you will never be alone.

March 16

Feeling like you're a burden to others

>>>>>>>

Today, I remind myself that asking for help does not make me a burden. I will allow myself to be supported, knowing that true connection comes from sharing both struggles and joys.

Have you ever felt like you're too much for the people around you? Like asking for help makes you a burden? I've felt that too.

But here's what I want you to remember: needing support doesn't make you a burden. Everyone needs support. Connection comes from sharing, both the highs and the lows. Let's remind each other that it's okay to lean on others.

We all struggle and suffer; You are not alone in it.

There is no shame in the struggle and suffering;

This is our one common bond.

You are enough; You are loved; You are worthy;

And you will never be alone.

March 17

Dealing with seasonal transitions (spring renewal)

>>>>>>>

Today, I will embrace the energy of renewal that spring brings. I will take steps to refresh my life, knowing that growth comes with change.

Spring is here, and with it comes the energy of renewal. But change can feel overwhelming sometimes, even when it's good.

Today, take one step toward refreshing your life. Maybe it's cleaning up your space, starting a new habit, or simply being present in the moment. Let's encourage each other by reminding that growth comes with change.

We all struggle and suffer; You are not alone in it.

There is no shame in the struggle and suffering;

This is our one common bond.

You are enough; You are loved; You are worthy;

And you will never be alone.

March 18

Struggling with unresolved grief

>>>>>>>

Today, I remind myself that grief is not a weakness. It's a reflection of love. I will allow myself to feel and heal at my own pace, knowing that I don't have to face this alone.

Grief can feel so isolating, like you are on an island that nobody knows about.   Like it's something you have to carry all by yourself. But here's what I want to remind you: grief isn't a weakness. It's love that still lingers.

Take the time you need to heal, to feel, to remember. You don't have to face this alone. Let's support each other in the weight of grief.

We all struggle and suffer; You are not alone in it.

There is no shame in the struggle and suffering;

This is our one common bond.

You are enough; You are loved; You are worthy;

And you will never be alone.

March 19

Struggling with fear of failure

>>>>>>>

Today, I remind myself that failure is not the opposite of success. It's part of the process. I will take one step forward, knowing that trying is a victory in itself.

Failure can feel like the end, can't it? Like proof that you weren't good enough. But failure isn't the opposite of success. Imagine that success is at the end of a long highway, and failure is just the lines that dot the road. It's part of how we get there.

Take one step today, even if it feels scary. Every attempt is a win, no matter the outcome. Let's remind each other that trying is always worth it.

We all struggle and suffer; You are not alone in it.

There is no shame in the struggle and suffering;

This is our one common bond.

You are enough; You are loved; You are worthy;

And you will never be alone.

March 20

Embracing growth and change

>>>>>>>

Today, I will embrace the changes in my life as opportunities for growth. I will trust in my ability to adapt and find strength in each step forward.

Change can be hard, can't it? Even when it's for the better, it can feel overwhelming. But here's what I want you to remember: growth doesn't happen without change.

Trust yourself to adapt, to find your footing, and to keep moving forward. Let's remind each other that change is how we grow.

We all struggle and suffer; You are not alone in it.

There is no shame in the struggle and suffering;

This is our one common bond.

You are enough; You are loved; You are worthy;

And you will never be alone.

March 21

Struggling with self-doubt

>>>>>>>

Today, I will remind myself that I am capable and resilient. I will focus on what I have overcome and trust in my ability to handle what comes next.

Self-doubt can creep in when you least expect it, can't it? That voice in your head saying, 'You're not enough.' But here's what I want you to remember: you are enough.

Think about what you've already overcome, the strength it took to get here. Trust yourself to keep moving forward. Let's remind each other that we're stronger than we think.

We all struggle and suffer; You are not alone in it.

There is no shame in the struggle and suffering;

This is our one common bond.

You are enough; You are loved; You are worthy;

And you will never be alone.

March 22

Feeling disconnected from personal goals

>>>>>>>

Today, I will take time to reconnect with my goals. I will reflect on what truly matters to me and take one small step toward creating the life I want.

Do you ever feel like you've lost touch with your goals? Like the things you once cared about feel so far away now? It's frustrating, isn't it?

But here's the thing. It's never too late to reconnect. Take a moment to reflect on what matters most to you, and take one small step in that direction. Let's remind each other that progress is always possible.

We all struggle and suffer; You are not alone in it.

There is no shame in the struggle and suffering;

This is our one common bond.

You are enough; You are loved; You are worthy;

And you will never be alone.

March 23

Coping with feelings of failure

>>>>>>>

Today, I will remind myself that failure is not final. I will focus on the lessons it offers and use them to keep moving forward.

Failure can feel so heavy, can't it? Like it's proof that you're not good enough. But remember that failure isn't the end. It's a lesson.

Think about what this experience can teach you, and use it to take your next step. You're not alone in this, and failure doesn't define you. Let's support each other as we keep moving forward.

We all struggle and suffer; You are not alone in it.

There is no shame in the struggle and suffering;

This is our one common bond.

You are enough; You are loved; You are worthy;

And you will never be alone.

March 24

Struggling with feelings of invisibility

\>>>>>>>

Today, I will remind myself that I matter, even if I feel unseen. I will seek out people and spaces where I am valued and remind myself of my own worth.

Do you ever feel invisible, like no one really sees you? It's a tough feeling, but here's what I want you to remember: you matter. Even if it feels like no one notices, your presence makes a difference.

Let's remind each other to seek out the people and places that see our value. You're not invisible here.

We all struggle and suffer; You are not alone in it.

There is no shame in the struggle and suffering;

This is our one common bond.

You are enough; You are loved; You are worthy;

And you will never be alone.

March 25

Struggling with loneliness during growth

>>>>>>>

Today, I remind myself that growth can feel lonely, but it's worth it. I will trust that the changes I'm making will lead me to stronger connections and a better future.

Growth can be lonely, can't it? When you're making changes, it can feel like the people around you don't understand. But here's what I want you to remember: growth is worth it.

The changes you're making now are leading you to something better. Trust that process, and remind yourself that you're not alone in this journey.

We all struggle and suffer; You are not alone in it.

There is no shame in the struggle and suffering;

This is our one common bond.

You are enough; You are loved; You are worthy;

And you will never be alone.

March 26

Struggling with fear of being vulnerable

>>>>>>>

Today, I will remind myself that vulnerability is a strength, not a weakness. I will take small steps to open up, knowing that honesty brings connection.

Being vulnerable can feel terrifying, can't it? Like you're exposing yourself to the risk of getting hurt. But here's the truth: vulnerability is how we connect.

Take one small step today to open up, whether it's sharing a thought, a feeling, or a part of your story. Let's remind each other that honesty is strength, not weakness.

We all struggle and suffer; You are not alone in it.

There is no shame in the struggle and suffering;

This is our one common bond.

You are enough; You are loved; You are worthy;

And you will never be alone.

March 27

Feeling stuck in toxic environments

>>>>>>>

Today, I remind myself that I have the power to create change. I will take steps to protect my peace and build an environment that supports my growth.

Toxic environments can feel suffocating, can't they? Like you're trapped with no way out. But here's the truth: you have the power to create change.

Start small. Set boundaries, seek support, or take a step toward something better. You deserve to be in spaces that uplift you. Let's remind each other that we're not stuck forever.

We all struggle and suffer; You are not alone in it.

There is no shame in the struggle and suffering;

This is our one common bond.

You are enough; You are loved; You are worthy;

And you will never be alone.

March 28

Struggling with shame over emotional struggles

>>>>>>>

Today, I remind myself that struggling emotionally is not something to be ashamed of. I will show myself compassion and seek support, knowing that healing takes courage.

Do you ever feel ashamed for struggling emotionally? Like you should have it all together? I've been there. But here's what I want you to remember: struggling doesn't mean you're weak. It means you're human.

Be kind to yourself today, and don't hesitate to reach out for support. Let's remind each other that healing takes courage.

We all struggle and suffer; You are not alone in it.

There is no shame in the struggle and suffering;

This is our one common bond.

You are enough; You are loved; You are worthy;

And you will never be alone.

March 29

Feeling disconnected from loved ones

>>>>>>>

Today, I will take steps to reconnect with the people who matter to me. I will reach out, knowing that meaningful relationships are built on effort and care.

Do you ever feel distant from the people you care about? Like you're not as close as you used to be? It's a tough place to be, but here's the thing: connection takes effort.

Reach out today, even if it's just a simple message. Let's remind each other that relationships are worth the work.

We all struggle and suffer; You are not alone in it.

There is no shame in the struggle and suffering;

This is our one common bond.

You are enough; You are loved; You are worthy;

And you will never be alone.

March 30

Struggling to find peace in uncertainty

>>>>>>>

Today, I remind myself that I don't have to have all the answers. I will focus on what I can control and trust that I am capable of navigating the unknown.

Uncertainty can feel overwhelming, can't it? Like you're stuck in the unknown with no clear path forward. But here's the truth: you don't have to have all the answers right now.

Focus on what you can control, and trust yourself to figure out the rest as you go. Let's remind each other that we're capable of navigating the unknown.

We all struggle and suffer; You are not alone in it.

There is no shame in the struggle and suffering;

This is our one common bond.

You are enough; You are loved; You are worthy;

And you will never be alone.

March 31

Celebrating progress and resilience

\>>>>>>>

Today, I will celebrate how far I've come. Even if the journey isn't perfect, I will honor my resilience and the strength it takes to keep going.

Take a moment today to look back at how far you've come. It's easy to focus on what's still ahead, but don't forget to honor the progress you've made.

You've been through so much, and you're still here. That's worth celebrating. Let's remind each other to appreciate our resilience.

We all struggle and suffer; You are not alone in it.

There is no shame in the struggle and suffering;

This is our one common bond.

You are enough; You are loved; You are worthy;

And you will never be alone.

April 1

Embracing opportunities for growth

>>>>>>>

Today, I remind myself that every challenge is an opportunity to grow. I will face the day with curiosity and openness, trusting that I am capable of learning and evolving.

Challenges can feel overwhelming, can't they? But here's the thing: every challenge is a chance to grow, to learn, and to become stronger.

Take today as an opportunity to face something with curiosity, even if it's tough. Growth doesn't happen all at once, but every step forward counts. Let's remind each other to keep growing.

We all struggle and suffer; You are not alone in it.

There is no shame in the struggle and suffering;

This is our one common bond.

You are enough; You are loved; You are worthy;

And you will never be alone.

April 2

Letting go of perfectionism

>>>>>>>

Today, I will remind myself that perfection is not the goal, progress is. I will allow myself to make mistakes, knowing that growth happens in the process.

Do you ever feel like everything has to be perfect before it's good enough? Like one mistake means you've failed? I've been there. But here's what I've learned: progress matters more than perfection.

Give yourself permission to make mistakes today. They're part of how we learn and grow. Let's remind each other that it's okay to be a work in progress.

We all struggle and suffer; You are not alone in it.

There is no shame in the struggle and suffering;

This is our one common bond.

You are enough; You are loved; You are worthy;

And you will never be alone.

April 3

Feeling overwhelmed by expectations

>>>>>>>

Today, I remind myself that I am not defined by others' expectations. I will set boundaries and focus on what feels right for me, knowing I deserve to live authentically.

Expectations can feel like a heavy weight, can't they? Whether they're from others or ourselves, they can be overwhelming. But here's what I want you to remember: you don't have to meet everyone else's expectations.

Focus on what feels right for you today. Set boundaries where you need to, and give yourself permission to live authentically. You're not alone in this.

We all struggle and suffer; You are not alone in it.

There is no shame in the struggle and suffering;

This is our one common bond.

You are enough; You are loved; You are worthy;

And you will never be alone.

April 4

Building self-confidence

>>>>>>>

Today, I will remind myself that confidence comes from within. I will celebrate my strengths and trust in my ability to handle whatever comes my way.

Confidence can feel hard to find sometimes, can't it? Like it's something you're supposed to have figured out already. But here's the truth: confidence isn't about being perfect. It's about trusting yourself.

Take a moment today to celebrate something you're good at, something you've accomplished. Let's remind each other that we all have strengths worth recognizing.

We all struggle and suffer; You are not alone in it.

There is no shame in the struggle and suffering;

This is our one common bond.

You are enough; You are loved; You are worthy;

And you will never be alone.

April 5

Coping with fear of change

>>>>>>>

Today, I remind myself that change is a natural part of life. I will embrace the opportunities it brings and trust in my ability to adapt and grow.

Change can feel scary, can't it? Even when it's for the better, it can feel like you're stepping into the unknown. But here's the truth: change is how we grow.

Trust yourself to handle what's ahead. Take it one step at a time, and remind yourself that you're capable of adapting. Let's support each other through life's changes.

We all struggle and suffer; You are not alone in it.

There is no shame in the struggle and suffering;

This is our one common bond.

You are enough; You are loved; You are worthy;

And you will never be alone.

April 6

Rediscovering joy in small moments

\>>>>>>>

Today, I will remind myself that joy is found in the present moment. I will look for the little things that bring light into my day and let myself feel gratitude for them.

Do you ever feel like joy is something you have to wait for? Like it only comes from big, life-changing moments? But here's the truth: joy is in the small things.

Take a moment today to notice something simple that makes you smile; a song, the weather, a kind word. Let's encourage each other to find joy in the present.

We all struggle and suffer; You are not alone in it.

There is no shame in the struggle and suffering;

This is our one common bond.

You are enough; You are loved; You are worthy;

And you will never be alone.

April 7

Overcoming the fear of being judged

>>>>>>>

Today, I remind myself that I am not defined by others' opinions. I will focus on being true to myself, knowing that authenticity is my greatest strength.

Fear of judgment can be paralyzing, can't it? It makes you second-guess everything you do. But here's what I've learned: other people's opinions don't define you.

Focus on being true to yourself today. The people who matter will value your authenticity. Let's remind each other to live authentically, without fear.

We all struggle and suffer; You are not alone in it.

There is no shame in the struggle and suffering;

This is our one common bond.

You are enough; You are loved; You are worthy;

And you will never be alone.

April 8

Feeling disconnected from community

>>>>>>>

Today, I will remind myself that connection takes effort, and that's okay. I will take one small step toward building or strengthening relationships that matter to me.

Do you ever feel like you're on the outside looking in? Like everyone else is connected, but you're not? It's a hard place to be, but here's the truth: connection takes effort.

Take one small step today; reach out, join something new, or just say hello. Let's encourage each other that we're all looking for connection.

We all struggle and suffer; You are not alone in it.

There is no shame in the struggle and suffering;

This is our one common bond.

You are enough; You are loved; You are worthy;

And you will never be alone.

April 9

Overcoming procrastination

>>>>>>>

Today, I will take one small step toward what I've been putting off. I will remind myself that progress is better than perfection and that action creates momentum.

Procrastination can feel like a cycle you can't break, can't it? The longer you wait, the harder it gets. But here's the thing: you don't have to do it all at once.

Even the smallest action can create momentum. Take one small step today. Let's remind each other that progress beats perfection every time.

We all struggle and suffer; You are not alone in it.

There is no shame in the struggle and suffering;

This is our one common bond.

You are enough; You are loved; You are worthy;

And you will never be alone.

April 10

Building emotional resilience

>>>>>>>

Today, I remind myself that resilience is not about never struggling. It's about getting back up. I will focus on my ability to learn, grow, and move forward, no matter what comes my way.

Resilience doesn't mean you never struggle. It means you keep going, even when things are hard.

Take a moment today to honor your resilience. You've overcome so much already, and you're capable of handling whatever comes next. Let's remind each other of our strength.

We all struggle and suffer; You are not alone in it.

There is no shame in the struggle and suffering;

This is our one common bond.

You are enough; You are loved; You are worthy;

And you will never be alone.

April 11

Coping with setbacks

>>>>>>>

Today, I remind myself that setbacks are not failures, but stepping stones. I will learn from them and use them to build a stronger foundation for my future.

Setbacks can feel like you're being pulled backward, can't they? Like all your progress is gone. But setbacks aren't failures, they're part of the process.

Take a moment to think about what you've learned from your challenges. Use that to take your next step forward. Let's remind each other that we're building something stronger.

We all struggle and suffer; You are not alone in it.

There is no shame in the struggle and suffering;

This is our one common bond.

You are enough; You are loved; You are worthy;

And you will never be alone.

April 12

Feeling unappreciated

\>>>>>>>

Today, I remind myself that my value is not dependent on recognition. I will seek out spaces and relationships where I am appreciated for who I am.

Do you ever feel like no one notices what you do? Like your efforts don't matter? It's a tough feeling, but here's what I want you to remember: your value isn't tied to recognition.
You are enough, just as you are. And the right people will see and appreciate that. Let's remind each other to find spaces where we're truly valued.

We all struggle and suffer; You are not alone in it.

There is no shame in the struggle and suffering;

This is our one common bond.

You are enough; You are loved; You are worthy;

And you will never be alone.

April 13

Struggling with comparison

>>>>>>>

Today, I will focus on my own journey. Comparing myself to others only distracts me from my progress. I will celebrate my growth and honor my unique path.

Comparison can steal your joy, can't it? You look at someone else's life and think, 'Why am I not there yet?' But here's the thing: their path isn't yours.

Celebrate the steps you've taken, no matter how small they seem. Your journey is unique, and it's valid. Let's remind each other that we're all growing at our own pace.

We all struggle and suffer; You are not alone in it.

There is no shame in the struggle and suffering;

This is our one common bond.

You are enough; You are loved; You are worthy;

And you will never be alone.

April 14

Struggling with self-doubt

>>>>>>>

Today, I remind myself that I am capable and strong. I will focus on what I've overcome and trust in my ability to handle whatever comes next.

Self-doubt can be so loud, can't it? That voice in your head saying, 'You can't do this.' But here's the truth: you've already overcome so much.

Take a moment today to think about your past victories, big or small. Let them remind you of your strength. Let's support each other in quieting self-doubt.

We all struggle and suffer; You are not alone in it.

There is no shame in the struggle and suffering;

This is our one common bond.

You are enough; You are loved; You are worthy;

And you will never be alone.

April 15

Overcoming guilt

>>>>>>>

Today, I will release the guilt I've been carrying. I will remind myself that I am human, and mistakes are part of growth. I deserve forgiveness, especially from myself.

Guilt can feel like a weight you can't put down, can't it? Like it's tied to you forever. But guilt is there because you are still growing. It means that you still care, and you still have something to work on.

Your mistakes don't define you. What matters is how you move forward. Let's remind each other to release that weight and focus on growth.

We all struggle and suffer; You are not alone in it.

There is no shame in the struggle and suffering;

This is our one common bond.

You are enough; You are loved; You are worthy;

And you will never be alone.

April 16

Fear of vulnerability

>>>>>>>

Today, I will remind myself that vulnerability is not weakness. It's courage. I will take small steps to share how I feel, knowing that openness builds connection.

Being vulnerable can feel terrifying, can't it? Like opening up is just asking to be hurt. But here's the truth: vulnerability isn't weakness. It's how we connect.

Take one small step today to share what you're feeling, even if it's just with someone you trust. Let's remind each other that honesty creates strength.

We all struggle and suffer; You are not alone in it.

There is no shame in the struggle and suffering;

This is our one common bond.

You are enough; You are loved; You are worthy;

And you will never be alone.

April 17

Embracing growth

>>>>>>>

Today, I will embrace the changes in my life as opportunities to grow. I will trust in my ability to adapt and find strength in every step forward.

Growth isn't always comfortable, is it? Sometimes it feels like everything is changing, and you're struggling to keep up. But here's what I've learned: growth comes with change.

Trust yourself to handle what's ahead. Take each step as it comes, and remind yourself that every step forward is progress. Let's remind each other that we're capable of growing through it all.

We all struggle and suffer; You are not alone in it.

There is no shame in the struggle and suffering;

This is our one common bond.

You are enough; You are loved; You are worthy;

And you will never be alone.

April 18

Feeling disconnected from loved ones

>>>>>>>

Today, I will take steps to reconnect with the people who matter to me. I will reach out, knowing that meaningful relationships require effort and care.

Do you ever feel distant from the people you care about? Like the connection isn't as strong as it used to be? It's a tough feeling, but here's the truth: relationships take effort.

Reach out today, even if it's just a small message or a kind word. Let's remind each other that connection is worth the work.

We all struggle and suffer; You are not alone in it.

There is no shame in the struggle and suffering;

This is our one common bond.

You are enough; You are loved; You are worthy;

And you will never be alone.

April 19

Feeling overwhelmed by responsibilities

>>>>>>>

Today, I will remind myself that I don't have to do everything at once. I will focus on what matters most and give myself grace for the rest.

Do you ever feel like the weight of everything you need to do is just too much? Like no matter how hard you try, it's never enough? I've been there.

But here's what I want you to remember: you don't have to do it all at once. Focus on what's most important, and give yourself permission to let the rest wait. Let's remind each other to take it one step at a time.

We all struggle and suffer; You are not alone in it.

There is no shame in the struggle and suffering;

This is our one common bond.

You are enough; You are loved; You are worthy;

And you will never be alone.

April 20

Rediscovering hope

>>>>>>>

Today, I will focus on the possibilities ahead. I will remind myself that even in difficult times, there is always room for hope and new beginnings.

Hope can feel hard to find sometimes, can't it? Especially when things aren't going the way you planned. But hope doesn't have to be big. It's okay for it to start small.

Look for one small thing today that gives you a reason to keep going. If nothing else, know that I care about you and want you to be here tomorrow. Let's encourage each other that there's always room for hope.

We all struggle and suffer; You are not alone in it.

There is no shame in the struggle and suffering;

This is our one common bond.

You are enough; You are loved; You are worthy;

And you will never be alone.

April 21

Finding peace in the present moment

>>>>>>>

Today, I will remind myself that the present moment is enough. I will let go of worries about the past and future, focusing on the peace I can create right now.

Do you ever feel like your mind is stuck in the past or racing ahead to the future? It's exhausting, isn't it? But here's the thing: the present moment is where we find peace.

Take a moment today to breathe, to notice what's around you, and to let yourself just be. Let's remind each other that we don't have to have it all figured out.

We all struggle and suffer; You are not alone in it.

There is no shame in the struggle and suffering;

This is our one common bond.

You are enough; You are loved; You are worthy;

And you will never be alone.

April 22

Struggling with self-worth

>>>>>>>

Today, I will remind myself that my worth is not determined by what I do or how others see me. I am enough, just as I am.

Self-worth can feel like a moving target, can't it? Like no matter what you do, it's never enough. But here's the truth: your worth isn't something you earn. It's something you already have.

Take a moment today to remind yourself that you're enough, just as you are. Let's support each other in seeing our own value.

We all struggle and suffer; You are not alone in it.

There is no shame in the struggle and suffering;

This is our one common bond.

You are enough; You are loved; You are worthy;

And you will never be alone.

April 23

Coping with feelings of loneliness

\>>>>>>>

Today, I remind myself that loneliness is a feeling, not a permanent state. I will take steps to connect with others, knowing that I am not alone in this experience.

Loneliness can feel so heavy, can't it? Like it's something you'll never escape. But here's what I want you to remember: loneliness is a feeling. It's not forever.

Take one small step today to connect, whether it's reaching out to someone, joining a group, or just saying hi. Let's remind each other that we're not alone in feeling this way.

We all struggle and suffer; You are not alone in it.

There is no shame in the struggle and suffering;

This is our one common bond.

You are enough; You are loved; You are worthy;

And you will never be alone.

April 24

Letting go of the need for control

>>>>>>>

Today, I will remind myself that I don't need to control everything to find peace. I will focus on what I can influence and let go of what I cannot.

Do you ever feel like you need to control everything around you to feel okay? Like if you let go, everything will fall apart? I've felt that too.

Peace doesn't come from control, it comes from trust. Focus on what you can influence, and let the rest go. Let's encourage each other to find peace in letting go.

We all struggle and suffer; You are not alone in it.

There is no shame in the struggle and suffering;

This is our one common bond.

You are enough; You are loved; You are worthy;

And you will never be alone.

April 25

Rediscovering joy in creativity

>>>>>>>

Today, I will remind myself that creativity is not about perfection. It's about expression. I will let myself create without judgment, knowing that joy comes from the process.

Do you ever feel like you're not creative because you're not 'good enough' at something? Like if it's not perfect, it doesn't count? But here's the thing: creativity isn't about being perfect. It's about expressing yourself.

Take a moment today to create something, just for the joy of it. Let's remind each other that there's no wrong way to be creative.

We all struggle and suffer; You are not alone in it.

There is no shame in the struggle and suffering;

This is our one common bond.

You are enough; You are loved; You are worthy;

And you will never be alone.

April 26

Finding purpose in small moments

\>>>>>>>

Today, I will remind myself that purpose doesn't have to be big or grand. I will find meaning in small moments and let them guide me toward a fulfilling life.

Do you ever feel like you're waiting for some big purpose to show up? Like life won't feel meaningful until you figure it out? But here's the truth: purpose is in the small moments.

It's in the kindness you show, the connections you make, and the way you live each day. Let's remind each other to find meaning in the little things.

We all struggle and suffer; You are not alone in it.

There is no shame in the struggle and suffering;

This is our one common bond.

You are enough; You are loved; You are worthy;

And you will never be alone.

April 27

Feeling stuck in routines

>>>>>>>

Today, I will remind myself that I have the power to make changes. I will take one small step to break out of my routine and create new energy in my life.

Routines can feel comforting, but sometimes they start to feel like a trap, don't they? Like you're stuck on repeat with no way out. But we all have the power to change. That includes you.

Take one small step today to try something new. Shake up your schedule or explore a different path. Let's remind each other that life doesn't have to feel so repetitive.

We all struggle and suffer; You are not alone in it.

There is no shame in the struggle and suffering;

This is our one common bond.

You are enough; You are loved; You are worthy;

And you will never be alone.

April 28

Celebrating resilience

\>>>>>>>

Today, I will honor my resilience. I will take a moment to reflect on the challenges I've faced and the strength it took to overcome them.

Take a moment today to think about everything you've been through. The challenges, the setbacks, the moments you weren't sure you'd make it through.

But here's the thing: you did. You're still here. Let's remind each other to celebrate our resilience and honor the strength it takes to keep going.

We all struggle and suffer; You are not alone in it.

There is no shame in the struggle and suffering;

This is our one common bond.

You are enough; You are loved; You are worthy;

And you will never be alone.

April 29

Overcoming fear of failure

>>>>>>>

Today, I remind myself that failure is not the end. It's a lesson. I will take one step forward, knowing that growth comes from trying.

Failure can feel like the end, can't it? Like proof that you're not good enough. But here's the truth: failure isn't the opposite of success. It's part of how we get there.

Take one step today, even if it feels scary. Growth comes from trying, no matter the outcome. Let's remind each other that failure is part of the journey.

We all struggle and suffer; You are not alone in it.

There is no shame in the struggle and suffering;

This is our one common bond.

You are enough; You are loved; You are worthy;

And you will never be alone.

April 30

Reflecting on progress

>>>>>>>

Today, I will reflect on how far I've come. I will celebrate my progress, no matter how small, and remind myself that growth is a journey, not a destination.

It's easy to focus on what's still ahead, but take a moment today to look back. Think about where you started, the progress you've made, and the strength it took to get here.

Celebrate that progress, no matter how small it feels. Let's remind each other that growth is a journey, and every step counts.

We all struggle and suffer; You are not alone in it.

There is no shame in the struggle and suffering;

This is our one common bond.

You are enough; You are loved; You are worthy;

And you will never be alone.

May 1

Embracing a fresh start

>>>>>>>

Today, I remind myself that each new month is an opportunity to begin again. I will let go of what no longer serves me and step forward with hope and purpose.

May is here, and it's the perfect time for a fresh start. Let this month be an opportunity to let go of what's been weighing you down and focus on what you want to grow.

You don't have to figure it all out today. Just take one small step toward something new. Let's remind each other that every month brings a chance to start fresh.

We all struggle and suffer; You are not alone in it.

There is no shame in the struggle and suffering;

This is our one common bond.

You are enough; You are loved; You are worthy;

And you will never be alone.

May 2

Finding courage in vulnerability

>>>>>>>

Today, I remind myself that vulnerability is not weakness. It's bravery. I will take a small step to open up, knowing that sharing my truth creates connection.

Being vulnerable is scary, isn't it? It feels like you're opening yourself up to risk. Here is what matters: vulnerability isn't weakness. It's how we connect.

Take a small step today. Share a thought, a feeling, or something on your mind. Let's remind each other that honesty builds bridges, not walls.

We all struggle and suffer; You are not alone in it.

There is no shame in the struggle and suffering;

This is our one common bond.

You are enough; You are loved; You are worthy;

And you will never be alone.

May 3

Rediscovering passion

>>>>>>>

Today, I will remind myself that my passions are worth pursuing. I will make time for what excites and inspires me, knowing that joy is found in the things that light me up.

Do you ever feel like you've lost touch with the things that once made you excited? Like your passions have taken a backseat? The reality is that it's never too late to rediscover them.

Take a moment today to do something that lights you up, no matter how small. Let's remind each other that our passions matter.

We all struggle and suffer; You are not alone in it.

There is no shame in the struggle and suffering;

This is our one common bond.

You are enough; You are loved; You are worthy;

And you will never be alone.

May 4

Coping with uncertainty

>>>>>>>

Today, I will remind myself that uncertainty is a natural part of life. I will trust in my ability to adapt and find peace in the unknown.

Uncertainty can feel so overwhelming, can't it? Like you're standing on shaky ground with no clear answers. But here's what I've learned: you don't have to have everything figured out right now.

Trust yourself to adapt, to handle what comes next. Let's remind each other that peace can be found, even in the unknown.

We all struggle and suffer; You are not alone in it.

There is no shame in the struggle and suffering;

This is our one common bond.

You are enough; You are loved; You are worthy;

And you will never be alone.

May 5

Feeling disconnected from joy

>>>>>>>

Today, I will remind myself that joy can be found in the simplest moments. I will look for reasons to smile and let myself fully experience them.

Joy can feel so far away sometimes, can't it? Like it's this big, unreachable thing. But underneath it all, joy isn't always grand. It's in the little things.

Take a moment today to notice something small that brings you happiness. Let's remind each other to look for joy, even in unexpected places.

We all struggle and suffer; You are not alone in it.

There is no shame in the struggle and suffering;

This is our one common bond.

You are enough; You are loved; You are worthy;

And you will never be alone.

May 6

Building resilience

\>\>\>\>\>\>\>

Today, I will remind myself that resilience is not about avoiding struggles. It's about how I rise after them. I will honor my strength and trust in my ability to keep moving forward.

Resilience isn't about never falling down. It's about getting back up, every single time.

Take a moment today to honor your strength, the way you've faced challenges and kept going. Let's remind each other that resilience is a journey, not a destination.

We all struggle and suffer; You are not alone in it.

There is no shame in the struggle and suffering;

This is our one common bond.

You are enough; You are loved; You are worthy;

And you will never be alone.

May 7

Overcoming fear of rejection

>>>>>>>

Today, I remind myself that rejection is not a reflection of my worth. I will take the risk to connect, knowing that I am worthy of love and belonging.

Rejection can feel like it's all about you, can't it? Like it's proof that you're not enough. But here's the truth: rejection doesn't define your worth. It's just part of life.

Take a step today to reach out, to connect, to try again. Let's remind each other that connection is worth the risk.

We all struggle and suffer; You are not alone in it.

There is no shame in the struggle and suffering;

This is our one common bond.

You are enough; You are loved; You are worthy;

And you will never be alone.

May 8

Struggling to let go of the past

>>>>>>>

Today, I will remind myself that the past does not define my future. I will honor what it taught me and focus on building a life that reflects who I am becoming.

Letting go of the past can feel impossible sometimes, can't it? Like it's holding onto you, even when you're ready to move on.

But here's the truth: the past is a lesson, not a life sentence. Take a step today to focus on what you're building, not what you've left behind. Let's remind each other that we're not defined by our past.

We all struggle and suffer; You are not alone in it.

There is no shame in the struggle and suffering;

This is our one common bond.

You are enough; You are loved; You are worthy;

And you will never be alone.

May 9

Struggling to ask for help

\>>>>>>>

Today, I will remind myself that asking for help is a strength, not a weakness. I will reach out, knowing that connection grows when we let others in.

Do you ever feel like asking for help makes you weak? Like you should be able to handle everything on your own? I've felt that too.

But here's the truth: asking for help takes courage. It's how we build connection and grow stronger together. Let's remind each other that we don't have to do it all alone.

We all struggle and suffer; You are not alone in it.

There is no shame in the struggle and suffering;

This is our one common bond.

You are enough; You are loved; You are worthy;

And you will never be alone.

May 10

Feeling stuck in routines

>>>>>>>

Today, I will remind myself that I have the power to create change. I will take one small step to bring new energy and excitement into my life.

Routines can feel comforting, but they can also start to feel like a trap, can't they? Like you're stuck on autopilot with no way out.

Take one small step today to shake things up; Try something new, change your schedule, or explore a new idea. Let's remind each other that life doesn't have to feel so repetitive.

We all struggle and suffer; You are not alone in it.

There is no shame in the struggle and suffering;

This is our one common bond.

You are enough; You are loved; You are worthy;

And you will never be alone.

May 11

Overcoming self-criticism

\>>>>>>>

Today, I will remind myself that I deserve the same kindness I offer others. I will speak to myself with compassion and focus on my progress, not my flaws.

Do you ever catch yourself being your own worst critic? Like you're harder on yourself than anyone else could ever be? I've been there too.

But here's the thing: you deserve the same kindness you show to others. Speak to yourself with compassion today, and focus on the progress you've made. Let's remind each other that we're all a work in progress.

We all struggle and suffer; You are not alone in it.

There is no shame in the struggle and suffering;

This is our one common bond.

You are enough; You are loved; You are worthy;

And you will never be alone.

May 12

Embracing imperfection

>>>>>>>

Today, I will let go of the need to be perfect. I will remind myself that imperfection is part of being human, and growth comes from embracing my flaws.

Perfection feels like the goal sometimes, doesn't it? But here's the truth: perfection isn't real. It's our imperfections that make us human, that help us grow.

Take a moment today to let go of the need to be perfect. Embrace the parts of you that are still learning. Let's remind each other that imperfection is beautiful.

We all struggle and suffer; You are not alone in it.

There is no shame in the struggle and suffering;

This is our one common bond.

You are enough; You are loved; You are worthy;

And you will never be alone.

May 13

Struggling with uncertainty in relationships

>>>>>>>

Today, I will remind myself that relationships take time and effort. I will trust in my ability to navigate uncertainty and build stronger connections.

Do you ever feel unsure about where you stand in a relationship? Like you don't know if you're doing enough or if they care as much as you do? It's tough, isn't it?

But here's what I've learned: relationships take time, effort, and trust. Take a step today to communicate, to show care, or to just be present. Let's remind each other that connection grows over time.

We all struggle and suffer; You are not alone in it.

There is no shame in the struggle and suffering;

This is our one common bond.

You are enough; You are loved; You are worthy;

And you will never be alone.

May 14

Dealing with fear of the future

>>>>>>>

Today, I will focus on the present moment. I will remind myself that I don't have to have all the answers for the future, but I am capable of handling whatever comes my way.

Do you ever feel like the future is just too big, too uncertain, too overwhelming? Like you can't figure out what's next? I've felt that too.

But here's the truth: you don't have to have it all figured out right now. Focus on what you can do today, and trust yourself to handle tomorrow when it comes. Let's remind each other that we're capable of navigating the unknown.

We all struggle and suffer; You are not alone in it.

There is no shame in the struggle and suffering;

This is our one common bond.

You are enough; You are loved; You are worthy;

And you will never be alone.

May 15

Rediscovering personal identity

>>>>>>>

Today, I will take time to reconnect with who I am. I will honor the things that bring me joy, peace, and purpose, knowing that my identity is always evolving.

Do you ever feel like you've lost touch with yourself? Like you're not sure who you are anymore? It's a tough place to be, but here's the thing: it's okay to rediscover yourself.

Take some time today to think about what brings you joy, what makes you feel at peace, what gives you purpose. Let's remind each other that identity is a journey, not a fixed destination.

We all struggle and suffer; You are not alone in it.

There is no shame in the struggle and suffering;

This is our one common bond.

You are enough; You are loved; You are worthy;

And you will never be alone.

May 16

Rebuilding trust in yourself

>>>>>>>

Today, I will remind myself that I can trust my own decisions. I will focus on what I've learned from the past and use it to guide me forward with confidence.

Do you ever doubt your own choices? Like you're afraid to trust yourself because of past mistakes? I've been there too.
But here's the truth: you've learned so much from what you've been through.

Trust that growth, and trust yourself to keep making progress. Let's remind each other that self-trust takes time, but it's worth building.

We all struggle and suffer; You are not alone in it.

There is no shame in the struggle and suffering;

This is our one common bond.

You are enough; You are loved; You are worthy;

And you will never be alone.

May 17

Finding balance between ambition and rest

>>>>>>>

Today, I will remind myself that rest is not the enemy of success. It's part of it. I will balance my ambition with care for my well-being.

Do you ever feel like you have to keep pushing, like rest is something you don't have time for? Like if you stop, you'll fall behind? I've felt that too.
But here's the truth: rest isn't the enemy of success. It's part of how we get there.

Take a moment today to breathe, to recharge, to remind yourself that balance matters. Let's support each other in finding that balance.

We all struggle and suffer; You are not alone in it.

There is no shame in the struggle and suffering;

This is our one common bond.

You are enough; You are loved; You are worthy;

And you will never be alone.

May 18

Feeling disconnected from personal goals

>>>>>>>

Today, I will take a small step to reconnect with my goals. I will remind myself that progress doesn't have to be perfect; It just has to move me forward.

Do you ever feel like your goals are slipping away, like they're not as clear as they used to be? It's easy to lose focus, but here's what I want you to remember: progress doesn't have to be perfect.

Take one small step today to reconnect with what matters to you. Let's remind each other that even small steps lead to big changes.

We all struggle and suffer; You are not alone in it.

There is no shame in the struggle and suffering;

This is our one common bond.

You are enough; You are loved; You are worthy;

And you will never be alone.

May 19

Overcoming fear of judgment

>>>>>>>

Today, I will remind myself that my life is my own. I will focus on living authentically, knowing that the opinions of others do not define me.

Fear of judgment can hold you back, can't it? It makes you second-guess yourself, wondering what people will think. But here's the truth: your life is yours to live.

Focus on what feels true to you today. The people who matter will respect your authenticity. Let's remind each other to live fully, without fear.

We all struggle and suffer; You are not alone in it.

There is no shame in the struggle and suffering;

This is our one common bond.

You are enough; You are loved; You are worthy;

And you will never be alone.

May 20

Celebrating small victories

>>>>>>>

Today, I will honor my progress, no matter how small. Every step forward is a win, and I will celebrate the strength it takes to keep going.

It's easy to overlook the small victories, isn't it? To think they're not worth celebrating because they're not 'big enough.' But here's the thing: every step forward is a win.

Take a moment today to celebrate something you've accomplished, no matter how small it feels. Let's remind each other that progress deserves recognition.

We all struggle and suffer; You are not alone in it.

There is no shame in the struggle and suffering;

This is our one common bond.

You are enough; You are loved; You are worthy;

And you will never be alone.

May 21

Letting go of what you can't control

>>>>>>>

Today, I will remind myself that I don't need to control everything to find peace. I will focus on what I can influence and release what is beyond my reach.

Do you ever feel like you're carrying the weight of things you can't control? Like no matter what you do, it's not enough? I've felt that too.

But here's the truth: peace doesn't come from control, it comes from letting go. Focus on what you can influence today, and trust yourself to handle the rest as it comes. Let's remind each other to let go of what we can't control.

We all struggle and suffer; You are not alone in it.

There is no shame in the struggle and suffering;

This is our one common bond.

You are enough; You are loved; You are worthy;

And you will never be alone.

May 22

Rebuilding confidence after setbacks

\>>>>>>>

Today, I will remind myself that setbacks do not define my worth. I will honor the strength it takes to keep going and trust in my ability to rebuild.

Setbacks can feel like they've knocked all the confidence out of you, can't they? Like everything you've built is gone. But here's the truth: a setback doesn't erase your progress.

Take a moment today to honor the strength it takes to start again. You're still moving forward, even when it feels slow. Let's remind each other that confidence grows with every step.

We all struggle and suffer; You are not alone in it.

There is no shame in the struggle and suffering;

This is our one common bond.

You are enough; You are loved; You are worthy;

And you will never be alone.

May 23

Finding joy in connection

>>>>>>>

Today, I will remind myself that connection brings joy. I will take a step to strengthen a relationship, knowing that we are meant to support and uplift each other.

Have you ever noticed how much lighter life feels when you connect with someone? Whether it's a deep conversation or just sharing a laugh, connection brings joy.

Take a moment today to reach out to someone. Text a friend, call a loved one, or even just smile at a stranger. Let's remind each other that joy grows in connection.

We all struggle and suffer; You are not alone in it.

There is no shame in the struggle and suffering;

This is our one common bond.

You are enough; You are loved; You are worthy;

And you will never be alone.

May 24

Overcoming fear of failure

>>>>>>>

Today, I will remind myself that failure is not the end. It's part of the journey. I will take one small step toward my goals, knowing that trying is a success in itself.

Fear of failure can be paralyzing, can't it? It whispers, 'What if you mess up? What if you're not good enough?' But here's the thing: failure isn't the end. It's a step on the path forward.

Take one small step today toward something you care about. Trying is a success all on its own. Let's remind each other that failure is how we grow.

We all struggle and suffer; You are not alone in it.

There is no shame in the struggle and suffering;

This is our one common bond.

You are enough; You are loved; You are worthy;

And you will never be alone.

May 25

Embracing curiosity

>>>>>>>

Today, I will remind myself that curiosity opens the door to possibility. I will approach the world with an open mind, ready to learn and grow.

Do you remember what it felt like to be curious as a kid? Like everything was new and full of possibility? Somewhere along the way, it's easy to lose that feeling.

Take a moment today to try something new, ask a question, or explore an idea. Curiosity brings growth, and it's never too late to rediscover it. Let's remind each other to stay open to life's possibilities.

We all struggle and suffer; You are not alone in it.

There is no shame in the struggle and suffering;

This is our one common bond.

You are enough; You are loved; You are worthy;

And you will never be alone.

May 26

Struggling with feelings of inadequacy

>>>>>>>

Today, I will remind myself that I am enough, just as I am. I will focus on my strengths and celebrate the unique qualities that make me who I am.

Do you ever feel like you're not enough? Like no matter what you do, it doesn't measure up? I've felt that too.

But here's the truth: you are enough, just as you are. Take a moment today to think about your strengths, the things that make you unique. Let's remind each other to see our own value.

We all struggle and suffer; You are not alone in it.

There is no shame in the struggle and suffering;

This is our one common bond.

You are enough; You are loved; You are worthy;

And you will never be alone.

May 27

Finding peace in stillness

>>>>>>>

Today, I will remind myself that it's okay to slow down. I will take time to be still, to reflect, and to find peace in the quiet moments.

Life moves fast, doesn't it? It feels like there's always something demanding your attention. But here's what I've learned: it's okay to slow down.

Take a moment today to be still; Breathe, reflect, and let yourself just be. Let's remind each other that peace is found in the quiet moments.

We all struggle and suffer; You are not alone in it.

There is no shame in the struggle and suffering;

This is our one common bond.

You are enough; You are loved; You are worthy;

And you will never be alone.

May 28

Honoring personal growth

\>>>>>>>

Today, I will celebrate the growth I've experienced, even if it feels small. I will remind myself that every step forward is a victory worth honoring.

It's easy to overlook your own growth, isn't it? To focus on what's still ahead instead of how far you've come.

Take a moment today to think about the progress you've made. Reflect on the lessons you've learned and the challenges you've overcome. Let's remind each other to celebrate every step forward.

We all struggle and suffer; You are not alone in it.

There is no shame in the struggle and suffering;

This is our one common bond.

You are enough; You are loved; You are worthy;

And you will never be alone.

May 29

Coping with grief during special occasions

>>>>>>>

Today, I will allow myself to feel whatever I need to feel. Special occasions can bring both joy and pain, and that's okay. I will honor my grief while staying open to moments of connection and peace.

Special occasions can be bittersweet when you're grieving. It's okay to miss them, to wish they were still here. But it's also okay to find moments of peace and connection, even in the pain.

Let's remind each other that grief and joy can coexist. You don't have to face these moments alone.

We all struggle and suffer; You are not alone in it.

There is no shame in the struggle and suffering;

This is our one common bond.

You are enough; You are loved; You are worthy;

And you will never be alone.

May 30

Building emotional resilience

>>>>>>>

Today, I will remind myself that resilience doesn't mean never struggling, it means continuing to move forward. I will honor my strength and trust in my ability to grow.

Emotional resilience isn't about having it all together, is it? It's about getting back up, even when it's hard.

Take a moment today to honor your strength, the way you've faced challenges and kept going. Let's remind each other that resilience is a journey, not a destination.

We all struggle and suffer; You are not alone in it.

There is no shame in the struggle and suffering;

This is our one common bond.

You are enough; You are loved; You are worthy;

And you will never be alone.

May 31

Reflecting on the month's progress

>>>>>>>

Today, I will reflect on the progress I've made this month. I will celebrate my victories, honor my resilience, and look forward to what lies ahead.

Take a moment today to look back at the month. Think about the challenges you've faced, the progress you've made, and the strength it took to get here.

Celebrate your victories, big or small, and honor your resilience. Let's remind each other that every step forward matters.

We all struggle and suffer; You are not alone in it.

There is no shame in the struggle and suffering;

This is our one common bond.

You are enough; You are loved; You are worthy;

And you will never be alone.

# June 1

Embracing new opportunities

>>>>>>>

Today, I will remind myself that every day is an opportunity to try something new. I will approach life with curiosity and openness, ready to embrace the possibilities ahead.

June is here, and it's the perfect time to step into something new. Life is full of possibilities, and today is an opportunity to try something you've never done before.

Whether it's a small change or a big adventure, take that step forward. Let's remind each other to embrace the unknown with curiosity.

We all struggle and suffer; You are not alone in it.

There is no shame in the struggle and suffering;

This is our one common bond.

You are enough; You are loved; You are worthy;

And you will never be alone.

June 2

Reconnecting with others

>>>>>>>

Today, I will take a step to reconnect with someone I care about. I will remind myself that relationships thrive on effort and openness.

Do you have someone in your life you've been meaning to reach out to? Maybe a friend you haven't talked to in a while, or someone you've drifted from.

Take a moment today to reconnect. Send that message, make that call; It might mean more to them than you realize. Let's remind each other that connection takes effort.

We all struggle and suffer; You are not alone in it.

There is no shame in the struggle and suffering;

This is our one common bond.

You are enough; You are loved; You are worthy;

And you will never be alone.

June 3

Trying something outside your comfort zone

>>>>>>>

Today, I will remind myself that growth happens when I step outside my comfort zone. I will try something new, even if it feels unfamiliar, trusting that I can handle the challenge.

Stepping outside your comfort zone can feel scary, can't it? Like you're taking a leap into the unknown. But here's the truth: that's where growth happens.

Try something new today. It doesn't have to be big. Even small steps lead to big changes. Let's remind each other to embrace the challenge.

We all struggle and suffer; You are not alone in it.

There is no shame in the struggle and suffering;

This is our one common bond.

You are enough; You are loved; You are worthy;

And you will never be alone.

June 4

Rediscovering joy in the little things

\>>>>>>>

Today, I will remind myself that joy can be found in the smallest moments. I will let myself notice and appreciate the little things that make life beautiful.

Sometimes, we get so caught up in the big picture that we forget about the little moments that bring us joy.

Take a moment today to notice something small. A laugh, a kind word, the way the sun feels on your skin. Let's remind each other to find joy in the little things.

We all struggle and suffer; You are not alone in it.

There is no shame in the struggle and suffering;

This is our one common bond.

You are enough; You are loved; You are worthy;

And you will never be alone.

June 5

Strengthening connections

\>>>>>>>

Today, I will focus on strengthening my connections with others. I will listen, share, and be present, knowing that relationships grow through intentional effort.

Relationships don't just happen, they grow when we take the time to nurture them.

Take a moment today to really listen to someone, to share something meaningful, or to just be present. Let's remind each other that connection takes care and effort.

We all struggle and suffer; You are not alone in it.

There is no shame in the struggle and suffering;

This is our one common bond.

You are enough; You are loved; You are worthy;

And you will never be alone.

June 6

Trusting yourself in the face of new challenges

>>>>>>>

Today, I will remind myself that I am capable of handling new challenges. I will trust in my strength, honor my progress, and face each new step with patience and confidence.

New challenges can feel overwhelming; like standing at the edge of something unfamiliar. Doubt whispers, "What if I'm not ready?" But you are more capable than you know.

You've faced hard things before. You've grown stronger, even when it didn't feel like it.

Take one small step today. It doesn't have to be perfect. It just has to be yours.

We all struggle and suffer; You are not alone in it.

There is no shame in the struggle and suffering;

This is our one common bond.

You are enough; You are loved; You are worthy;

And you will never be alone.

June 7

Exploring new possibilities

>>>>>>>

Today, I will allow myself to explore new possibilities. I will remind myself that life is full of opportunities waiting to be discovered.

Have you ever wondered what could happen if you just tried something new? Life is full of possibilities, and sometimes, all it takes is a little curiosity to open a new door.

Take a moment today to explore; Try a new hobby, take a different route, or just let yourself dream. Let's remind each other to stay curious.

We all struggle and suffer; You are not alone in it.

There is no shame in the struggle and suffering;

This is our one common bond.

You are enough; You are loved; You are worthy;

And you will never be alone.

June 8

Building meaningful friendships

>>>>>>>

Today, I will take steps to build or strengthen meaningful friendships. I will remind myself that connections grow through kindness, effort, and shared experiences.

Friendships aren't always easy to build, are they? But here's the truth: the best ones are worth the effort.

Take a moment today to reach out to someone, to make plans, or to share a meaningful moment. Let's remind each other that friendships grow when we care for them.

We all struggle and suffer; You are not alone in it.

There is no shame in the struggle and suffering;

This is our one common bond.

You are enough; You are loved; You are worthy;

And you will never be alone.

June 9

Celebrating progress

>>>>>>>

Today, I will honor the progress I've made, no matter how small. Every step forward is a victory, and I will celebrate my journey.

It's easy to overlook your progress, isn't it? To focus on what's left to do instead of how far you've come.

Take a moment today to celebrate the steps you've taken, big or small. Let's remind each other that every bit of progress matters.

We all struggle and suffer; You are not alone in it.

There is no shame in the struggle and suffering;

This is our one common bond.

You are enough; You are loved; You are worthy;

And you will never be alone.

June 10

Embracing life's adventure

>>>>>>>

Today, I will embrace life as an adventure. I will approach each moment with curiosity, courage, and a sense of wonder.

Life can feel like a routine sometimes, but what if we looked at it as an adventure?

Take a moment today to see the world through curious eyes. Try something new, take a different perspective, or just appreciate the journey. Let's remind each other to embrace life's adventure.

We all struggle and suffer; You are not alone in it.

There is no shame in the struggle and suffering;

This is our one common bond.

You are enough; You are loved; You are worthy;

And you will never be alone.

June 11

Finding courage to take the first step

>>>>>>>

Today, I will remind myself that the first step is the hardest, but also the most important. I will face my fears and trust in my ability to move forward.

Starting something new can feel overwhelming, can't it? Like the first step is just too big. But here's the thing: once you take that first step, the path starts to unfold.

Trust yourself to take that step today. It doesn't have to be perfect, it just has to be yours. Let's remind each other that beginnings are brave.

We all struggle and suffer; You are not alone in it.

There is no shame in the struggle and suffering;

This is our one common bond.

You are enough; You are loved; You are worthy;

And you will never be alone.

June 12

Discovering new passions

>>>>>>>

Today, I will allow myself to explore what excites and inspires me. I will remind myself that it's never too late to discover a new passion.

Do you ever feel like it's too late to try something new? Like you should've found your passion already? But here's the truth: it's never too late to discover something that lights you up.

Take a moment today to explore; Try a new hobby, learn something new, or follow a curiosity. Let's remind each other that passion can be found at any time.

We all struggle and suffer; You are not alone in it.

There is no shame in the struggle and suffering;

This is our one common bond.

You are enough; You are loved; You are worthy;

And you will never be alone.

June 13

Letting go of comparison

\>>>>>>>

Today, I will remind myself that my journey is my own. I will focus on my growth and celebrate my unique path without comparing it to others.

Comparison is so easy, isn't it? You look at someone else's life and think, 'Why am I not there yet?' But here's the thing: their path isn't yours.

Celebrate where you are today, and trust that your journey is unfolding the way it's meant to. Let's remind each other to honor our unique paths.

We all struggle and suffer; You are not alone in it.

There is no shame in the struggle and suffering;

This is our one common bond.

You are enough; You are loved; You are worthy;

And you will never be alone.

June 14

Building trust in relationships

>>>>>>>

Today, I will focus on building trust in my relationships. I will show up with honesty and openness, knowing that strong connections are built over time.

Trust doesn't happen overnight, does it? It's something we build, step by step, through honesty and care.

Take a moment today to strengthen trust in one of your relationships. Listen, share, or simply be present. Let's remind each other that connection grows with time and effort.

We all struggle and suffer; You are not alone in it.

There is no shame in the struggle and suffering;

This is our one common bond.

You are enough; You are loved; You are worthy;

And you will never be alone.

June 15

Reclaiming your voice

>>>>>>>

Today, I will remind myself that my voice matters. I will speak with confidence, knowing that what I have to say is worth sharing.

Do you ever feel like your voice doesn't matter? Like what you have to say isn't worth sharing? But here's the truth: your voice matters.

Speak up today. Share your thoughts, express your feelings, or stand up for what you believe in. Let's remind each other that our voices deserve to be heard.

We all struggle and suffer; You are not alone in it.

There is no shame in the struggle and suffering;

This is our one common bond.

You are enough; You are loved; You are worthy;

And you will never be alone.

June 16

Overcoming fear of change

>>>>>>>

Today, I will embrace change as an opportunity to grow. I will remind myself that I am capable of adapting and finding strength in the process.

Change can feel so overwhelming, can't it? Like you're being pushed into the unknown with no map. But here's the truth: change is how we grow.

Take a moment today to see change as an opportunity instead of a challenge. Let's remind each other that we're capable of adapting and thriving.

We all struggle and suffer; You are not alone in it.

There is no shame in the struggle and suffering;

This is our one common bond.

You are enough; You are loved; You are worthy;

And you will never be alone.

June 17

Rediscovering joy in connection

>>>>>>>

Today, I will focus on the joy that comes from connection. I will take time to engage with others, knowing that shared moments bring light to life.

Have you ever noticed how much joy connection brings? Whether it's a deep conversation or just sharing a laugh, being with others makes life brighter.

Take a moment today to connect; call a friend, spend time with someone you care about, or just reach out. Let's remind each other that joy grows in connection.

We all struggle and suffer; You are not alone in it.

There is no shame in the struggle and suffering;

This is our one common bond.

You are enough; You are loved; You are worthy;

And you will never be alone.

June 18

Exploring self-discovery

>>>>>>>

Today, I will take time to explore who I am becoming. I will embrace the process of self-discovery, knowing that growth is a lifelong journey.

Do you ever feel like you're still figuring yourself out? Like you're a work in progress? That's okay; self-discovery is a journey, not a destination.

Take some time today to reflect on who you are and who you want to become. Let's remind each other that it's okay to keep learning about ourselves.

We all struggle and suffer; You are not alone in it.

There is no shame in the struggle and suffering;

This is our one common bond.

You are enough; You are loved; You are worthy;

And you will never be alone.

June 19

Celebrating courage in small actions

>>>>>>>

Today, I will honor the courage it takes to try. I will remind myself that even small steps require bravery, and every effort is worth celebrating.

Trying something new, speaking up, or taking a step forward. Those small actions take courage, don't they? It's easy to overlook how brave they are.

Take a moment today to celebrate your courage, no matter how small the action. Let's remind each other that bravery comes in many forms.

We all struggle and suffer; You are not alone in it.

There is no shame in the struggle and suffering;

This is our one common bond.

You are enough; You are loved; You are worthy;

And you will never be alone.

June 20

Finding freedom in curiosity

>>>>>>>

Today, I will let curiosity guide me. I will remind myself that exploring new ideas and perspectives brings freedom and growth.

Curiosity has a way of opening doors, doesn't it? It helps you see the world differently, to explore ideas you never thought of before.

Take a moment today to follow your curiosity. Ask questions, try something new, or learn about something that interests you. Let's remind each other that curiosity leads to growth.

We all struggle and suffer; You are not alone in it.

There is no shame in the struggle and suffering;

This is our one common bond.

You are enough; You are loved; You are worthy;

And you will never be alone.

June 21

Embracing the present moment

>>>>>>>

Today, I will focus on the present moment. I will let go of past regrets and future worries, finding peace and joy in what is here and now.

Do you ever find yourself stuck in the past or worrying about the future? It's easy to forget about the moment we're living in right now.

Take a moment today to pause and be fully present. Notice what's around you, breathe deeply, and let yourself just be. Let's remind each other that peace is found in the present.

We all struggle and suffer; You are not alone in it.

There is no shame in the struggle and suffering;

This is our one common bond.

You are enough; You are loved; You are worthy;

And you will never be alone.

June 22

Reconnecting with nature

>>>>>>>

Today, I will take time to connect with nature. I will let the beauty of the world around me inspire calm and remind me of the bigger picture.

When was the last time you really noticed nature? The way the trees sway, the feel of the sun or breeze, the sound of birds?

Take a moment today to step outside and reconnect. Nature has a way of reminding us that we're part of something bigger. Let's remind each other to slow down and appreciate it.

We all struggle and suffer; You are not alone in it.

There is no shame in the struggle and suffering;

This is our one common bond.

You are enough; You are loved; You are worthy;

And you will never be alone.

June 23

Strengthening self-trust

>>>>>>>

Today, I will trust myself. I will remind myself that I have the knowledge and resilience to make decisions that support my growth and happiness.

Do you ever second-guess yourself, wondering if you're making the right choices? It's easy to doubt, but here's the truth: you've learned so much from your journey so far.

Trust yourself today; your instincts, your knowledge, your ability to adapt. Let's remind each other that self-trust is built one step at a time.

We all struggle and suffer; You are not alone in it.

There is no shame in the struggle and suffering;

This is our one common bond.

You are enough; You are loved; You are worthy;

And you will never be alone.

June 24

Rediscovering wonder

>>>>>>>

Today, I will remind myself to see the world with wonder. I will let curiosity and awe guide me, finding beauty in the everyday.

Do you remember what it was like to see the world through a child's eyes? Everything felt new, full of wonder.

Take a moment today to rediscover that feeling. Notice the little details, the things you might take for granted. Let's remind each other to find beauty in the everyday.

We all struggle and suffer; You are not alone in it.

There is no shame in the struggle and suffering;

This is our one common bond.

You are enough; You are loved; You are worthy;

And you will never be alone.

June 25

Deepening meaningful relationships

\>>>>>>>

Today, I will nurture my relationships. I will be present, listen deeply, and share openly, knowing that meaningful connections require care.

Have you ever noticed how much stronger relationships feel when you're fully present? When you take the time to really listen and share?

Take a moment today to nurture one of your relationships. Whether it's with a friend, family member, or someone new. Let's remind each other that meaningful connections grow with care.

We all struggle and suffer; You are not alone in it.

There is no shame in the struggle and suffering;

This is our one common bond.

You are enough; You are loved; You are worthy;

And you will never be alone.

June 26

Exploring new perspectives

>>>>>>>

Today, I will open my mind to new perspectives. I will remind myself that learning from others helps me grow and see the world in new ways.

Do you ever feel like you're stuck seeing things the same way? Sometimes, all it takes is hearing someone else's perspective to spark something new.

Take a moment today to listen to someone's story, read about something unfamiliar, or just ask questions. Let's remind each other that new perspectives help us grow.

We all struggle and suffer; You are not alone in it.

There is no shame in the struggle and suffering;

This is our one common bond.

You are enough; You are loved; You are worthy;

And you will never be alone.

June 27

Honoring personal achievements

>>>>>>>

Today, I will celebrate my achievements, big and small. I will remind myself that every success is a reflection of my effort and resilience.

It's easy to overlook your achievements, isn't it? To focus on what's next instead of celebrating what you've already done.

Take a moment today to honor your successes, no matter how small they seem. Let's remind each other that every win is worth celebrating.

We all struggle and suffer; You are not alone in it.

There is no shame in the struggle and suffering;

This is our one common bond.

You are enough; You are loved; You are worthy;

And you will never be alone.

June 28

Finding freedom in letting go

>>>>>>>

Today, I will remind myself that letting go creates space for new opportunities. I will release what no longer serves me and focus on what brings me peace.

Letting go can feel hard, can't it? Like you're losing something, even if it's not helping you anymore. But here's the truth: letting go makes room for something better.

Take a moment today to release one thing that's been weighing you down. Let's remind each other that letting go creates space for growth.

We all struggle and suffer; You are not alone in it.

There is no shame in the struggle and suffering;

This is our one common bond.

You are enough; You are loved; You are worthy;

And you will never be alone.

June 29

Taking joy in the journey

>>>>>>>

Today, I will remind myself that life is about the journey, not just the destination. I will find joy in the steps I take and celebrate the path I'm on.

It's easy to get so focused on where you're going that you forget to enjoy the journey, isn't it?

Take a moment today to appreciate the steps you're taking. The progress, the lessons, and the little joys along the way. Let's remind each other to find happiness in the journey.

We all struggle and suffer; You are not alone in it.

There is no shame in the struggle and suffering;

This is our one common bond.

You are enough; You are loved; You are worthy;

And you will never be alone.

June 30

Reflecting on the month's growth

>>>>>>>

Today, I will take time to reflect on how I've grown this month. I will honor the lessons I've learned and look forward to the opportunities ahead.

As June comes to a close, take a moment to look back. Think about the challenges you've faced, the steps you've taken, and the growth you've experienced.

Celebrate how far you've come, and look ahead with hope. Let's remind each other that every month is a chance to grow.

We all struggle and suffer; You are not alone in it.

There is no shame in the struggle and suffering;

This is our one common bond.

You are enough; You are loved; You are worthy;

And you will never be alone.

July 1

Embracing independence

>>>>>>>

Today, I will remind myself that I am capable of standing on my own. I will celebrate my independence and trust in my ability to create the life I want.

Independence is a powerful thing, isn't it? It's the ability to trust yourself, to take steps toward the life you want.

Take a moment today to celebrate how far you've come on your own. Remind yourself that you're capable of so much. Let's honor our independence together.

We all struggle and suffer; You are not alone in it.

There is no shame in the struggle and suffering;

This is our one common bond.

You are enough; You are loved; You are worthy;

And you will never be alone.

July 2

Finding strength in challenges

>>>>>>>

Today, I will remind myself that challenges are opportunities to grow. I will face them with courage and trust in my strength to overcome them.

Challenges can feel overwhelming, can't they? Like they're pushing you to your limit. But here's the truth: every challenge is an opportunity to grow stronger.

Take a moment today to see your struggles as stepping stones. Trust yourself to rise above them. Let's remind each other of our strength in the face of challenges.

We all struggle and suffer; You are not alone in it.

There is no shame in the struggle and suffering;

This is our one common bond.

You are enough; You are loved; You are worthy;

And you will never be alone.

July 3

Setting boundaries

>>>>>>>

Today, I will remind myself that setting boundaries is an act of self-respect. I will honor my needs and create space for what matters most.

Do you ever feel guilty about setting boundaries? Like you're letting people down by saying no? Here's the thing: boundaries aren't selfish; they're self-respect.

Take a moment today to honor your needs and set one boundary that brings you peace. Let's remind each other that boundaries create healthier relationships.

We all struggle and suffer; You are not alone in it.

There is no shame in the struggle and suffering;

This is our one common bond.

You are enough; You are loved; You are worthy;

And you will never be alone.

July 4

Celebrating freedom

>>>>>>>

Today, I will celebrate the freedom to choose my path. I will honor the journey I am on and the opportunities I have to grow and thrive.

Freedom comes in many forms. The freedom to make your own choices, to grow, and to change your path.

Take a moment today to celebrate the choices you've made and the opportunities ahead. Let's remind each other that freedom is a gift worth honoring.

We all struggle and suffer; You are not alone in it.

There is no shame in the struggle and suffering;

This is our one common bond.

You are enough; You are loved; You are worthy;

And you will never be alone.

July 5

Building inner strength

>>>>>>>

Today, I will focus on my inner strength. I will remind myself that I have the resilience to face anything life brings my way.

Inner strength is something we all have, but sometimes it's easy to forget it's there.

Take a moment today to reflect on the challenges you've overcome and the strength it took to keep going. Let's remind each other that we are resilient.

We all struggle and suffer; You are not alone in it.

There is no shame in the struggle and suffering;

This is our one common bond.

You are enough; You are loved; You are worthy;

And you will never be alone.

July 6

Trusting yourself

>>>>>>>

Today, I will trust myself to make decisions that align with my values and goals. I will honor my intuition and believe in my ability to move forward.

Do you ever doubt your own decisions? Like you're afraid of making the wrong choice? I've been there.
But here's the truth: you've come this far because of the choices you've made.

Trust yourself to keep moving forward. Let's remind each other to honor our intuition.

We all struggle and suffer; You are not alone in it.

There is no shame in the struggle and suffering;

This is our one common bond.

You are enough; You are loved; You are worthy;

And you will never be alone.

July 7

Embracing resilience

>>>>>>>

Today, I will remind myself that resilience is not about never falling. It's about rising every time I do. I will honor my ability to keep going, no matter what.

Resilience isn't about being perfect or never struggling. It's about getting back up, no matter how many times you fall.

Take a moment today to honor your resilience. You've faced challenges before, and you'll rise again. Let's remind each other that we are stronger than we know.

We all struggle and suffer; You are not alone in it.

There is no shame in the struggle and suffering;

This is our one common bond.

You are enough; You are loved; You are worthy;

And you will never be alone.

July 8

Prioritizing self-care

>>>>>>>

Today, I will remind myself that taking care of myself is not selfish. It's necessary. I will make time for rest, reflection, and the things that bring me peace.

Self-care can feel like a luxury sometimes, but here's the truth: it's not selfish. It's necessary.

Take a moment today to prioritize yourself, whether it's a walk, a break, or something that makes you happy. Let's remind each other that taking care of ourselves helps us show up stronger.

We all struggle and suffer; You are not alone in it.

There is no shame in the struggle and suffering;

This is our one common bond.

You are enough; You are loved; You are worthy;

And you will never be alone.

July 9

Letting go of self-doubt

>>>>>>>

Today, I will let go of self-doubt and embrace self-confidence. I will remind myself that I am capable, worthy, and ready to succeed.

Self-doubt can be so loud, can't it? That voice that tells you you're not ready or not good enough. But here's the thing: you are capable.

Take a moment today to quiet that voice and replace it with confidence. Let's remind each other to believe in ourselves.

We all struggle and suffer; You are not alone in it.

There is no shame in the struggle and suffering;

This is our one common bond.

You are enough; You are loved; You are worthy;

And you will never be alone.

July 10

Celebrating small victories

>>>>>>>

Today, I will celebrate my small victories. I will remind myself that every step forward, no matter how small, is worth honoring.

It's easy to overlook the small victories, isn't it? To think they don't matter as much as the big wins.
But here's the truth: every step forward is a step worth celebrating.

Take a moment today to honor your progress, no matter how small. Let's remind each other to celebrate the little things.

We all struggle and suffer; You are not alone in it.

There is no shame in the struggle and suffering;

This is our one common bond.

You are enough; You are loved; You are worthy;

And you will never be alone.

July 11

Finding joy in independence

>>>>>>>

Today, I will celebrate my independence. I will remind myself that standing on my own is an opportunity to grow and thrive.

Independence can feel empowering, but it can also feel a little lonely at times. Here's the truth: it's a chance to grow and discover what you're capable of.

Take a moment today to celebrate the things you've accomplished on your own. Let's remind each other that independence is a strength.

We all struggle and suffer; You are not alone in it.

There is no shame in the struggle and suffering;

This is our one common bond.

You are enough; You are loved; You are worthy;

And you will never be alone.

July 12

Building emotional resilience

>>>>>>>

Today, I will remind myself that resilience is about how I rise after I fall. I will honor my ability to keep moving forward, no matter what.

Life will knock us down sometimes. That's just the way it is. But here's what I've learned: resilience is about how you get back up.

Take a moment today to reflect on the times you've risen after a fall. Let's remind each other that resilience is something we all have within us.

We all struggle and suffer; You are not alone in it.

There is no shame in the struggle and suffering;

This is our one common bond.

You are enough; You are loved; You are worthy;

And you will never be alone.

July 13

Trusting the process

>>>>>>>

Today, I will trust that I am on the right path. I will remind myself that growth takes time and that every step forward is meaningful.

Do you ever feel like you're not moving fast enough or like progress is too slow? Here's the thing: growth takes time.

Trust that you're on the right path, even if it feels slow. Every step forward matters, no matter how small. Let's remind each other to trust the process.

We all struggle and suffer; You are not alone in it.

There is no shame in the struggle and suffering;

This is our one common bond.

You are enough; You are loved; You are worthy;

And you will never be alone.

July 14

Letting go of what doesn't serve you

>>>>>>>

Today, I will release what no longer serves me. I will make space for new opportunities and experiences that align with my values.

Sometimes, we hold onto things; habits, relationships, or fears that don't serve us anymore. Letting go can feel hard, but it's also freeing.

Take a moment today to release one thing that's been weighing you down. Let's remind each other that letting go creates space for something better.

We all struggle and suffer; You are not alone in it.

There is no shame in the struggle and suffering;

This is our one common bond.

You are enough; You are loved; You are worthy;

And you will never be alone.

July 15

Celebrating your uniqueness

>>>>>>>

Today, I will celebrate the qualities that make me unique. I will remind myself that my individuality is my strength and my gift to the world.

Do you ever feel like you're not enough because you're different? Like you don't fit the mold? Here's the truth: your uniqueness is your strength.

Take a moment today to celebrate what makes you, you. Let's remind each other that individuality is a gift.

We all struggle and suffer; You are not alone in it.

There is no shame in the struggle and suffering;

This is our one common bond.

You are enough; You are loved; You are worthy;

And you will never be alone.

July 16

Honoring your progress

>>>>>>>

Today, I will honor how far I've come. I will remind myself that every step I've taken is proof of my strength and resilience.

It's easy to get caught up in where you want to go and forget about how far you've come.

Take a moment today to reflect on the progress you've made. The challenges you've overcome, the lessons you've learned. Let's remind each other to celebrate our journeys.

We all struggle and suffer; You are not alone in it.

There is no shame in the struggle and suffering;

This is our one common bond.

You are enough; You are loved; You are worthy;

And you will never be alone.

July 17

Cultivating self-compassion

>>>>>>>

Today, I will treat myself with the same kindness I show others. I will remind myself that self-compassion is a vital part of growth.

Do you ever find yourself being harder on yourself than you'd ever be on someone else? Like you don't deserve the same kindness?

Take a moment today to offer yourself the compassion you freely give others. Let's remind each other that growth thrives on self-kindness.

We all struggle and suffer; You are not alone in it.

There is no shame in the struggle and suffering;

This is our one common bond.

You are enough; You are loved; You are worthy;

And you will never be alone.

July 18

Strengthening your voice

>>>>>>>

Today, I will remind myself that my voice matters. I will speak with confidence, knowing that what I have to say is important.

Do you ever feel like your voice doesn't matter? Like what you have to say isn't worth sharing? Here's the truth: your voice is powerful.

Take a moment today to share your thoughts, stand up for something you believe in, or just speak from the heart. Let's remind each other that our voices are valuable.

We all struggle and suffer; You are not alone in it.

There is no shame in the struggle and suffering;

This is our one common bond.

You are enough; You are loved; You are worthy;

And you will never be alone.

July 19

Rediscovering joy in everyday moments

>>>>>>>

Today, I will look for joy in the small, everyday moments. I will remind myself that happiness is often found in the simplest things.

Joy doesn't always come from big, life-changing events. Sometimes, it's in the smallest moments like a kind word, a favorite song, or a quiet evening.

Take a moment today to notice and appreciate something simple that brings you joy. Let's remind each other that happiness is often found in the little things.

We all struggle and suffer; You are not alone in it.

There is no shame in the struggle and suffering;

This is our one common bond.

You are enough; You are loved; You are worthy;

And you will never be alone.

July 20

Standing tall in your independence

>>>>>>>

Today, I will honor the independence I've worked to build. I will remind myself that standing tall on my own is a reflection of my strength.

Independence can feel empowering, but it's also something you work for. It's the small decisions, the steps forward, the times you didn't give up.

Take a moment today to honor how far you've come on your own. Let's remind each other that independence is strength.

We all struggle and suffer; You are not alone in it.

There is no shame in the struggle and suffering;

This is our one common bond.

You are enough; You are loved; You are worthy;

And you will never be alone.

July 21

Embracing personal growth

>>>>>>>

Today, I will remind myself that growth is a lifelong journey. I will honor the changes I've made and trust the process of becoming my best self.

Personal growth isn't a destination. It's a journey. There's no finish line where everything is perfect.

Take a moment today to honor the progress you've made, even if it feels small. Let's remind each other that growth is constant, and every step matters.

We all struggle and suffer; You are not alone in it.

There is no shame in the struggle and suffering;

This is our one common bond.

You are enough; You are loved; You are worthy;

And you will never be alone.

July 22

Finding peace in imperfection

>>>>>>>

Today, I will let go of the need to be perfect. I will remind myself that imperfection is part of being human, and it's through flaws that I grow.

Do you ever feel like you have to have everything together all the time? Like perfection is the only option? Here's the truth: no one is perfect, and that's okay.

Take a moment today to let go of that pressure and embrace the beauty in your imperfections. Let's remind each other that flaws are part of the journey.

We all struggle and suffer; You are not alone in it.

There is no shame in the struggle and suffering;

This is our one common bond.

You are enough; You are loved; You are worthy;

And you will never be alone.

July 23

Focusing on your inner strength

>>>>>>>

Today, I will remind myself that my strength comes from within. I will trust in my resilience and believe in my ability to overcome challenges.

Strength isn't just about how much you can handle. It's about what's inside you. It's the resilience you show, the hope you hold onto, the way you keep going.

Take a moment today to recognize that strength within yourself. Let's remind each other that we're stronger than we realize.

We all struggle and suffer; You are not alone in it.

There is no shame in the struggle and suffering;

This is our one common bond.

You are enough; You are loved; You are worthy;

And you will never be alone.

July 24

Reclaiming your time and energy

>>>>>>>

Today, I will focus on reclaiming my time and energy. I will remind myself that it's okay to say no and to prioritize what truly matters to me.

Do you ever feel like your time and energy are being pulled in a million directions? Like you're saying yes to everything but yourself?

Take a moment today to reclaim that space. Set a boundary, say no, or focus on what matters most to you. Let's remind each other that it's okay to prioritize ourselves.

We all struggle and suffer; You are not alone in it.

There is no shame in the struggle and suffering;

This is our one common bond.

You are enough; You are loved; You are worthy;

And you will never be alone.

July 25

Celebrating your resilience

>>>>>>>

Today, I will celebrate my resilience. I will remind myself that every challenge I've faced has made me stronger and more capable.

Resilience is something we don't always notice in ourselves, but it's there. It's in the way you've overcome challenges, kept going, and grown along the way.

Take a moment today to celebrate your resilience. The strength it takes to keep moving forward. Let's remind each other of how far we've come.

We all struggle and suffer; You are not alone in it.

There is no shame in the struggle and suffering;

This is our one common bond.

You are enough; You are loved; You are worthy;

And you will never be alone.

July 26

Finding joy in simplicity

>>>>>>>

Today, I will remind myself that joy doesn't have to be big or complicated. I will find happiness in the simple moments and let them fill my day with light.

Joy is often found in the simplest moments, like a quiet cup of coffee, a walk outside, or a favorite song.

Take a moment today to slow down and appreciate something small that brings you happiness. Let's remind each other that simplicity often holds the greatest joy.

We all struggle and suffer; You are not alone in it.

There is no shame in the struggle and suffering;

This is our one common bond.

You are enough; You are loved; You are worthy;

And you will never be alone.

July 27

Strengthening your sense of purpose

>>>>>>>

Today, I will focus on what gives my life purpose. I will remind myself that even small actions contribute to a life of meaning and fulfillment.

Purpose doesn't have to be something big or life-changing. It can be found in small, everyday actions.

Take a moment today to think about what gives your life meaning, whether it's helping others, creating something, or just being present. Let's remind each other that purpose is personal and powerful.

We all struggle and suffer; You are not alone in it.

There is no shame in the struggle and suffering;

This is our one common bond.

You are enough; You are loved; You are worthy;

And you will never be alone.

July 28

Trusting in your progress

>>>>>>>

Today, I will trust in the progress I'm making. I will remind myself that growth takes time and that every step forward is meaningful.

It's easy to feel like you're not moving fast enough, isn't it? Like progress should be quicker or bigger. But here's the thing: growth takes time.

Take a moment today to trust in the steps you've taken, no matter how small. Let's remind each other that progress is progress.

We all struggle and suffer; You are not alone in it.

There is no shame in the struggle and suffering;

This is our one common bond.

You are enough; You are loved; You are worthy;

And you will never be alone.

July 29

Releasing fear of judgment

\>>>>>>>

Today, I will let go of the fear of being judged. I will remind myself that my worth is not determined by others' opinions but by how I see and value myself.

Fear of judgment can be so heavy, can't it? It makes you second-guess yourself, hold back, and dim your light.
But here's the truth: your worth isn't tied to what others think.

Take a moment today to focus on how you see yourself. Let's remind each other that self-worth comes from within.

We all struggle and suffer; You are not alone in it.

There is no shame in the struggle and suffering;

This is our one common bond.

You are enough; You are loved; You are worthy;

And you will never be alone.

July 30

Celebrating your individuality

>>>>>>>

Today, I will celebrate the unique person I am. I will remind myself that my individuality is my greatest strength and my gift to the world.

Your individuality is what makes you, you. It's your story, your strengths, your perspective. It's what makes you stand out.

Take a moment today to celebrate your unique qualities. Let's remind each other that our individuality is something to be proud of.

We all struggle and suffer; You are not alone in it.

There is no shame in the struggle and suffering;

This is our one common bond.

You are enough; You are loved; You are worthy;

And you will never be alone.

July 31

Reflecting on your journey

>>>>>>>

Today, I will reflect on how far I've come this month. I will honor the challenges I've faced, the victories I've achieved, and the lessons I've learned.

As July comes to a close, take a moment to look back. Think about the challenges you've faced, the progress you've made, and the strength it took to keep going.

Celebrate your growth, and look forward to what's next. Let's remind each other that every step forward matters.

We all struggle and suffer; You are not alone in it.

There is no shame in the struggle and suffering;

This is our one common bond.

You are enough; You are loved; You are worthy;

And you will never be alone.

August 1

Embracing new beginnings

>>>>>>>

Today, I will remind myself that every day is a fresh start. I will let go of yesterday's worries and step into the possibilities of today.

August is here, and it's the perfect time for a fresh start. Let go of the weight of yesterday, and focus on the possibilities ahead.

Take a moment today to embrace something new. It could be an idea, a habit, or just a positive thought. Let's remind each other that every day brings a chance to begin again.

We all struggle and suffer; You are not alone in it.

There is no shame in the struggle and suffering;

This is our one common bond.

You are enough; You are loved; You are worthy;

And you will never be alone.

August 2

Focusing on your goals

>>>>>>>

Today, I will realign with my goals. I will remind myself that progress takes focus and that every small step brings me closer to where I want to be.

Do you ever feel like your goals have drifted out of focus? Like you're not sure where you're headed anymore?

Take a moment today to realign. Think about what you want, and take one small step toward it. Let's remind each other that progress is built step by step.

We all struggle and suffer; You are not alone in it.

There is no shame in the struggle and suffering;

This is our one common bond.

You are enough; You are loved; You are worthy;

And you will never be alone.

August 3

Letting go of distractions

>>>>>>>

Today, I will let go of distractions that don't serve me. I will focus on what truly matters and invest my time in things that bring me peace and purpose.

It's so easy to get caught up in distractions, isn't it? The little things that pull you away from what really matters.

Take a moment today to refocus. Let go of one thing that doesn't serve you. Let's remind each other to prioritize what brings us peace and purpose.

We all struggle and suffer; You are not alone in it.

There is no shame in the struggle and suffering;

This is our one common bond.

You are enough; You are loved; You are worthy;

And you will never be alone.

August 4

Cultivating patience

\>>>>>>>

Today, I will practice patience with myself and my journey. I will remind myself that growth takes time and that every step forward is meaningful.

Do you ever feel like you're not moving fast enough? Like growth should happen overnight? Here's the truth: real change takes time.

Be patient with yourself today. Trust that every step forward matters, even the small ones. Let's remind each other that patience is part of the process.

We all struggle and suffer; You are not alone in it.

There is no shame in the struggle and suffering;

This is our one common bond.

You are enough; You are loved; You are worthy;

And you will never be alone.

August 5

Reconnecting with your purpose

>>>>>>>

Today, I will take time to reflect on my purpose. I will remind myself that even small actions contribute to a meaningful life.

Have you ever felt disconnected from your purpose? Like you're just going through the motions?

Take a moment today to think about what gives your life meaning. Whether it's helping others, creating, or simply being present. Let's remind each other that purpose is found in the everyday.

We all struggle and suffer; You are not alone in it.

There is no shame in the struggle and suffering;

This is our one common bond.

You are enough; You are loved; You are worthy;

And you will never be alone.

August 6

Embracing change

>>>>>>>

Today, I will remind myself that change is an opportunity for growth. I will trust in my ability to adapt and find strength in new beginnings.

Change can feel uncomfortable, can't it? Like stepping into the unknown with no guarantees. But here's the truth: change is how we grow.

Take a moment today to embrace one small change, and trust that you're capable of adapting. Let's remind each other that growth comes from trying something new.

We all struggle and suffer; You are not alone in it.

There is no shame in the struggle and suffering;

This is our one common bond.

You are enough; You are loved; You are worthy;

And you will never be alone.

August 7

Practicing self-discipline instead of motivation

>>>>>>>

Today, I will commit to self-discipline. I will remind myself that small, consistent actions build the foundation for success and I take those actions every day, even when I don't feel like it.

It's easy to do hard things when we feel motivated, but motivation doesn't always come easy, does it? That's why it's more important to build self-discipline. It's about choosing the small, meaningful actions over the easier distractions.

Take a moment today to commit to one habit, one task, or one step toward your goal. Let's remind each other that consistency is key to success.

We all struggle and suffer; You are not alone in it.

There is no shame in the struggle and suffering;

This is our one common bond.

You are enough; You are loved; You are worthy;

And you will never be alone.

August 8

Releasing perfectionism

>>>>>>>

Today, I will remind myself that progress is more important than perfection. I will celebrate my efforts, knowing that mistakes are part of growth.

Do you ever feel like if it's not perfect, it's not worth doing? Like every mistake sets you back? Here's the truth: progress, not perfection, is what matters.

Take a moment today to celebrate your efforts, even if they're not perfect. Let's remind each other that growth comes from trying.

We all struggle and suffer; You are not alone in it.

There is no shame in the struggle and suffering;

This is our one common bond.

You are enough; You are loved; You are worthy;

And you will never be alone.

August 9

Building meaningful habits

>>>>>>>

Today, I will focus on building habits that support my growth. I will remind myself that consistency creates change and that small actions add up over time.

Habits are the building blocks of change, but starting them can feel overwhelming, can't it?

Take a moment today to focus on one habit (just one) that supports your growth. Let's remind each other that small actions add up over time.

We all struggle and suffer; You are not alone in it.

There is no shame in the struggle and suffering;

This is our one common bond.

You are enough; You are loved; You are worthy;

And you will never be alone.

August 10

Finding clarity in your priorities

>>>>>>>

Today, I will take time to clarify my priorities. I will focus on what aligns with my values and let go of what distracts me from my goals.

Do you ever feel like your priorities are all over the place? Like you're pulled in too many directions?

Take a moment today to focus on what matters most to you. Let go of one thing that doesn't align with your goals. Let's remind each other to stay clear and focused.

We all struggle and suffer; You are not alone in it.

There is no shame in the struggle and suffering;

This is our one common bond.

You are enough; You are loved; You are worthy;

And you will never be alone.

August 11

Strengthening self-trust

>>>>>>>

Today, I will remind myself that I can trust my decisions. I will honor my intuition and believe in my ability to choose what's best for me.

Do you ever second-guess yourself, wondering if you're making the right choice? It's hard, isn't it? But here's the thing: you've already made countless good decisions to get to where you are.

Take a moment today to trust your intuition and believe in yourself. Let's remind each other that self-trust is powerful.

We all struggle and suffer; You are not alone in it.

There is no shame in the struggle and suffering;

This is our one common bond.

You are enough; You are loved; You are worthy;

And you will never be alone.

August 12

Overcoming procrastination

>>>>>>>

Today, I will take one small step toward what I've been putting off. I will remind myself that action creates momentum, and every little bit counts.

Procrastination can feel like a mountain, can't it? The longer you wait, the bigger the task seems. But here's the truth: action creates momentum.

Take one small step today. It doesn't have to be perfect, just started. Let's remind each other that every little bit counts.

We all struggle and suffer; You are not alone in it.

There is no shame in the struggle and suffering;

This is our one common bond.

You are enough; You are loved; You are worthy;

And you will never be alone.

August 13

Finding balance

>>>>>>>

Today, I will focus on finding balance in my life. I will remind myself that it's okay to rest, and I will prioritize what brings me peace and fulfillment.

Do you ever feel like you're juggling too much, like there's no space for you? Balance can feel impossible sometimes, but here's the truth: it's okay to rest.

Take a moment today to prioritize one thing that brings you peace. Let's remind each other that balance is part of the journey.

We all struggle and suffer; You are not alone in it.

There is no shame in the struggle and suffering;

This is our one common bond.

You are enough; You are loved; You are worthy;

And you will never be alone.

August 14

Letting go of what no longer serves you

>>>>>>>

Today, I will release what no longer aligns with my goals or values. I will create space for the things that bring me growth and happiness.

Letting go can feel hard, can't it? Like you're giving up something, even if it doesn't serve you anymore. But here's the truth: letting go creates space for something better.

Take a moment today to release one thing that no longer aligns with your values. Let's remind each other that growth comes from making room for it.

We all struggle and suffer; You are not alone in it.

There is no shame in the struggle and suffering;

This is our one common bond.

You are enough; You are loved; You are worthy;

And you will never be alone.

August 15

Celebrating your progress

>>>>>>>

Today, I will honor the progress I've made, no matter how small. I will remind myself that each step forward is a victory worth celebrating.

It's easy to focus on what's still ahead and forget how far you've come, isn't it?

Take a moment today to celebrate your progress. Whether it's big or small, it matters. Let's remind each other that every step forward is worth honoring.

We all struggle and suffer; You are not alone in it.

There is no shame in the struggle and suffering;

This is our one common bond.

You are enough; You are loved; You are worthy;

And you will never be alone.

August 16

Strengthening meaningful connections

>>>>>>>

Today, I will focus on deepening my relationships. I will show up with kindness, listen with intention, and create space for genuine connection.

Relationships thrive when we give them care and attention. Whether it's a friend, a family member, or someone new, connection takes effort.

Take a moment today to reach out, listen, or show kindness. Let's remind each other that meaningful relationships are worth nurturing.

We all struggle and suffer; You are not alone in it.

There is no shame in the struggle and suffering;

This is our one common bond.

You are enough; You are loved; You are worthy;

And you will never be alone.

August 17

Trusting the process of growth

>>>>>>>

Today, I will remind myself that growth is not always linear. I will trust the process and honor the progress I've made along the way.

Growth can feel frustrating sometimes, can't it? Like you're taking one step forward and two steps back. But here's the truth: growth isn't always a straight line.

Take a moment today to trust the process and honor where you are. Let's remind each other that progress comes in many forms.

We all struggle and suffer; You are not alone in it.

There is no shame in the struggle and suffering;

This is our one common bond.

You are enough; You are loved; You are worthy;

And you will never be alone.

August 18

Rediscovering your passion

>>>>>>>

Today, I will allow myself to explore what excites and inspires me. I will remind myself that passion can be rediscovered at any time.

Do you ever feel like you've lost touch with what used to excite you? Like your passions have taken a back seat?

Take a moment today to rediscover one thing that inspires you. Whether it's an old hobby or something new. Let's remind each other that it's never too late to reignite passion.

We all struggle and suffer; You are not alone in it.

There is no shame in the struggle and suffering;

This is our one common bond.

You are enough; You are loved; You are worthy;

And you will never be alone.

August 19

Building self-discipline

>>>>>>>

Today, I will focus on building habits that align with my goals. I will remind myself that self-discipline is a form of self-respect and a path to success.

Discipline isn't about being hard on yourself. It's about respecting your goals and your time.

Take a moment today to commit to one habit or action that moves you closer to where you want to be. Let's remind each other that discipline creates freedom.

We all struggle and suffer; You are not alone in it.

There is no shame in the struggle and suffering;

This is our one common bond.

You are enough; You are loved; You are worthy;

And you will never be alone.

August 20

Reconnecting with the present moment

>>>>>>>

Today, I will remind myself that the present moment is enough. I will let go of past regrets and future worries to focus on the here and now.

Do you ever feel stuck in the past or anxious about the future? Like the present moment just slips by unnoticed?

Take a moment today to ground yourself in the here and now. Breathe, observe, and let yourself simply be. Let's remind each other that the present is where life happens.

We all struggle and suffer; You are not alone in it.

There is no shame in the struggle and suffering;

This is our one common bond.

You are enough; You are loved; You are worthy;

And you will never be alone.

August 21

Embracing new opportunities

>>>>>>>

Today, I will remain open to new opportunities. I will remind myself that stepping into the unknown can lead to growth and exciting possibilities.

Opportunities often come when we least expect them, don't they? But stepping into the unknown can feel scary.

Take a moment today to stay open to something new. It could be a conversation, a project, or just an idea. Let's remind each other that opportunities bring growth.

We all struggle and suffer; You are not alone in it.

There is no shame in the struggle and suffering;

This is our one common bond.

You are enough; You are loved; You are worthy;

And you will never be alone.

August 22

Releasing fear of failure

>>>>>>>

Today, I will let go of the fear of failure. I will remind myself that every attempt is a step toward success and that mistakes are opportunities to learn.

Fear of failure can hold you back, can't it? It makes you question whether trying is even worth it. But here's the truth: every mistake is a chance to learn.

Take one step today, even if it feels uncertain. Let's remind each other that failure is just part of the journey.

We all struggle and suffer; You are not alone in it.

There is no shame in the struggle and suffering;

This is our one common bond.

You are enough; You are loved; You are worthy;

And you will never be alone.

August 23

Strengthening your focus

>>>>>>>

Today, I will focus my energy on what truly matters. I will let go of distractions and invest in the things that align with my goals and values.

Do you ever feel like your energy is being pulled in too many directions? Like distractions are everywhere?

Take a moment today to refocus. Choose one thing that aligns with your goals and give it your attention. Let's remind each other to stay clear and intentional.

We all struggle and suffer; You are not alone in it.

There is no shame in the struggle and suffering;

This is our one common bond.

You are enough; You are loved; You are worthy;

And you will never be alone.

August 24

Finding peace in stillness

>>>>>>>

Today, I will take time to be still and present. I will remind myself that peace is found in slowing down and embracing the moment.

Life moves fast, doesn't it? It's easy to feel like there's no time to stop and breathe. But here's the truth: peace is found in stillness.

Take a moment today to pause, breathe deeply, reflect, and just be present. Let's remind each other that slowing down can bring clarity.

We all struggle and suffer; You are not alone in it.

There is no shame in the struggle and suffering;

This is our one common bond.

You are enough; You are loved; You are worthy;

And you will never be alone.

August 25

Honoring your strengths

>>>>>>>

Today, I will celebrate my strengths. I will remind myself that my unique qualities and abilities are what make me resilient and capable.

It's easy to focus on what you're not good at, isn't it? But what about the things you're great at? The strengths that make you, you?

Take a moment today to acknowledge one of your strengths, and let it remind you of how capable you are. Let's remind each other to honor what makes us strong.

We all struggle and suffer; You are not alone in it.

There is no shame in the struggle and suffering;

This is our one common bond.

You are enough; You are loved; You are worthy;

And you will never be alone.

August 26

Letting go of self-doubt

>>>>>>>

Today, I will let go of self-doubt and embrace self-belief. I will remind myself that I am capable and deserving of success.

Self-doubt can be loud, can't it? It whispers, 'You're not ready' or 'You're not good enough.' But here's the truth: you are capable.

Take a moment today to quiet that doubt and replace it with belief in yourself. Let's remind each other that self-belief is powerful.

We all struggle and suffer; You are not alone in it.

There is no shame in the struggle and suffering;

This is our one common bond.

You are enough; You are loved; You are worthy;

And you will never be alone.

August 27

Celebrating small victories

>>>>>>>

Today, I will honor the small victories in my life. I will remind myself that every step forward, no matter how small, is worth celebrating.

It's easy to overlook the little wins, isn't it? To focus only on the big milestones. But here's the truth: every step forward is a victory.

Take a moment today to celebrate something small you've achieved. Let's remind each other that progress is worth celebrating.

We all struggle and suffer; You are not alone in it.

There is no shame in the struggle and suffering;

This is our one common bond.

You are enough; You are loved; You are worthy;

And you will never be alone.

August 28

Building meaningful habits

>>>>>>>

Today, I will focus on building habits that support my growth. I will remind myself that consistency creates change and that small actions lead to big results.

Good habits don't happen overnight, do they? They're built one small action at a time.

Take a moment today to focus on one habit that supports your growth. Even the smallest step makes a difference. Let's remind each other that consistency is key.

We all struggle and suffer; You are not alone in it.

There is no shame in the struggle and suffering;

This is our one common bond.

You are enough; You are loved; You are worthy;

And you will never be alone.

August 29

Trusting your journey

>>>>>>>

Today, I will remind myself that my journey is unique. I will trust the path I'm on and believe that I'm moving toward the life I want.

It's easy to compare your journey to someone else's, isn't it? To feel like you're not where you 'should' be. But here's the thing: your path is yours alone.

Take a moment today to trust your progress and believe in your direction. Let's remind each other that every journey is unique.

We all struggle and suffer; You are not alone in it.

There is no shame in the struggle and suffering;

This is our one common bond.

You are enough; You are loved; You are worthy;

And you will never be alone.

August 30

Reflecting on your growth

>>>>>>>

Today, I will take time to reflect on my growth this month. I will honor the challenges I've faced, the progress I've made, and the lessons I've learned.

As August comes to a close, take a moment to look back. Think about the challenges you've faced, the steps you've taken, and the progress you've made.

Celebrate your growth, and let it motivate you for what's next. Let's remind each other to honor our journeys.

We all struggle and suffer; You are not alone in it.

There is no shame in the struggle and suffering;

This is our one common bond.

You are enough; You are loved; You are worthy;

And you will never be alone.

August 31

Preparing for new beginnings

>>>>>>>

Today, I will look ahead with hope and excitement. I will remind myself that every ending is the start of something new and full of possibilities.

August is ending, but that doesn't mean the journey stops. Every ending is a chance for a new beginning, for new opportunities.

Take a moment today to look forward with hope and excitement for what's to come. Let's remind each other that the best is yet to come.

We all struggle and suffer; You are not alone in it.

There is no shame in the struggle and suffering;

This is our one common bond.

You are enough; You are loved; You are worthy;

And you will never be alone.

September 1

Embracing change

>>>>>>>

Today, I will remind myself that change is a natural part of life. I will trust in my ability to adapt and find opportunities in new beginnings.

September is here, and with it comes a season of change. Change can feel uncertain, can't it? But it's also full of possibility.

Take a moment today to embrace one change in your life, no matter how small. Let's remind each other that change brings growth.

We all struggle and suffer; You are not alone in it.

There is no shame in the struggle and suffering;

This is our one common bond.

You are enough; You are loved; You are worthy;

And you will never be alone.

September 2

Finding balance in transitions

>>>>>>>

Today, I will focus on finding balance during times of transition. I will remind myself that I can navigate change with grace and strength.

Transitions can feel overwhelming, can't they? Like everything is shifting at once. But here's the truth: balance is possible, even in the midst of change.

Take a moment today to focus on one thing that grounds you, something that keeps you steady. Let's remind each other that we can navigate change with strength.

We all struggle and suffer; You are not alone in it.

There is no shame in the struggle and suffering;

This is our one common bond.

You are enough; You are loved; You are worthy;

And you will never be alone.

September 3

Honoring your progress

>>>>>>>

Today, I will honor how far I've come. I will remind myself that even during times of change, I am growing and moving forward.

Do you ever feel like you're not making progress? Like change is just throwing you off track? But here's the thing: even in transitions, you're still growing.

Take a moment today to reflect on how far you've come and the strength it's taken to get here. Let's remind each other to celebrate our progress.

We all struggle and suffer; You are not alone in it.

There is no shame in the struggle and suffering;

This is our one common bond.

You are enough; You are loved; You are worthy;

And you will never be alone.

September 4

Strengthening connections

>>>>>>>

Today, I will focus on strengthening my relationships. I will remind myself that meaningful connections require care and effort.

Relationships can feel harder to maintain during busy or changing times, can't they? But meaningful connections are worth the effort.

Take a moment today to reach out to someone. Send a message, make a call, or just show up. Let's remind each other that relationships thrive with care.

We all struggle and suffer; You are not alone in it.

There is no shame in the struggle and suffering;

This is our one common bond.

You are enough; You are loved; You are worthy;

And you will never be alone.

September 5

Trusting the process of growth

>>>>>>>

Today, I will trust the process of growth. I will remind myself that even when it feels slow, every step forward is meaningful.

Growth can feel frustrating, especially when it doesn't happen as quickly as you'd like. But here's the truth: progress doesn't have to be fast to be meaningful.

Take a moment today to trust where you're headed, even if the steps feel small. Let's remind each other that growth is a process.

We all struggle and suffer; You are not alone in it.

There is no shame in the struggle and suffering;

This is our one common bond.

You are enough; You are loved; You are worthy;

And you will never be alone.

September 6

Finding joy in change

>>>>>>>

Today, I will look for joy in the changes around me. I will remind myself that even in uncertainty, there are moments of beauty and growth.

Change can feel like a whirlwind, can't it? But if you slow down, there's joy to be found in the process; new opportunities, unexpected beauty, growth.

Take a moment today to notice something positive about a change in your life. Let's remind each other that joy can be found, even in uncertainty.

We all struggle and suffer; You are not alone in it.

There is no shame in the struggle and suffering;

This is our one common bond.

You are enough; You are loved; You are worthy;

And you will never be alone.

September 7

Letting go of fear

>>>>>>>

Today, I will let go of fear and embrace courage. I will remind myself that I am stronger than my doubts and capable of facing challenges.

Fear has a way of holding you back, doesn't it? It whispers, 'What if you fail?' or 'What if you're not enough?' But here's the truth: you are stronger than your fears.

Take a moment today to face one small fear and remind yourself of your strength. Let's remind each other that courage is within us.

We all struggle and suffer; You are not alone in it.

There is no shame in the struggle and suffering;

This is our one common bond.

You are enough; You are loved; You are worthy;

And you will never be alone.

September 8

Celebrating small victories

>>>>>>>

Today, I will celebrate the small victories in my life. I will remind myself that every step forward, no matter how small, is worth honoring.

It's easy to overlook the little wins, isn't it? To think they're not as important as the big milestones. But here's the truth: every step forward matters.

Take a moment today to celebrate something small you've achieved. Let's remind each other that progress deserves recognition.

We all struggle and suffer; You are not alone in it.

There is no shame in the struggle and suffering;

This is our one common bond.

You are enough; You are loved; You are worthy;

And you will never be alone.

September 9

Reconnecting with your values

>>>>>>>

Today, I will take time to reconnect with my values. I will remind myself that my choices are guided by what matters most to me.

Do you ever feel like life pulls you in directions that don't align with who you are? Like you're moving away from what truly matters?

Take a moment today to reflect on your values and let them guide your next steps. Let's remind each other to live in alignment with what we care about.

We all struggle and suffer; You are not alone in it.

There is no shame in the struggle and suffering;

This is our one common bond.

You are enough; You are loved; You are worthy;

And you will never be alone.

September 10

Finding strength in community

>>>>>>>

Today, I will remind myself that I am not alone. I will reach out and find strength in the support and connection of others.

Sometimes, it's easy to feel like you have to do it all on your own, isn't it? Like asking for help means you're weak. But here's the truth: strength is found in community.

Take a moment today to reach out; whether it's sharing, listening, or just being present. Let's remind each other that connection gives us strength.

We all struggle and suffer; You are not alone in it.

There is no shame in the struggle and suffering;

This is our one common bond.

You are enough; You are loved; You are worthy;

And you will never be alone.

September 11

Supporting others with kindness

\>>>>>>>

Today, I will remind myself that a simple act of kindness can make a difference. I will show up for others, especially the men in my life, and remind them they're not alone.

Sometimes, the strongest thing we can do is show up for someone else. A text, a call, even just listening can remind someone they matter.

Take a moment today to check in on a friend, especially a man in your life who might be struggling. Let's remind each other that we're here for one another.

We all struggle and suffer; You are not alone in it.

There is no shame in the struggle and suffering;

This is our one common bond.

You are enough; You are loved; You are worthy;

And you will never be alone.

September 12

Prioritizing your mental health

>>>>>>>

Today, I will prioritize my mental health. I will remind myself that taking care of my mind is just as important as taking care of my body.

Mental health isn't talked about enough, especially for men. But here's the truth: it's just as important as your physical health.

Take a moment today to check in with yourself. Are you resting? Talking about what's on your mind? Let's remind each other that mental health matters.

We all struggle and suffer; You are not alone in it.

There is no shame in the struggle and suffering;

This is our one common bond.

You are enough; You are loved; You are worthy;

And you will never be alone.

September 13

Embracing vulnerability

\>>>>>>>

Today, I will remind myself that vulnerability is not a weakness. It's a strength. I will open up about how I feel and create space for others to do the same.

Being vulnerable can feel uncomfortable, can't it? Like you're opening yourself up to judgment. But here's the thing: vulnerability creates connection.

Take a moment today to share something real with someone you trust. Let's remind each other that being open is a strength.

We all struggle and suffer; You are not alone in it.

There is no shame in the struggle and suffering;

This is our one common bond.

You are enough; You are loved; You are worthy;

And you will never be alone.

September 14

Breaking the stigma around mental health

>>>>>>>

Today, I will remind myself that it's okay to talk about mental health. By sharing my story, I help break the stigma and create space for others to do the same.

Men don't talk about mental health enough, do we? There's this stigma, this pressure to 'man up.' But here's the truth: talking about it is what makes us stronger.

Take a moment today to share how you're feeling or ask someone how they're doing. Let's remind each other that it's okay to talk.

We all struggle and suffer; You are not alone in it.

There is no shame in the struggle and suffering;

This is our one common bond.

You are enough; You are loved; You are worthy;

And you will never be alone.

September 15

Finding strength in asking for help

\>>>>>>>

Today, I will remind myself that asking for help is not a weakness. It's a sign of strength. I will reach out when I need support and encourage others to do the same.

Do you ever feel like asking for help means you're failing? Like you should be able to handle everything on your own? Here's the truth: asking for help is brave.

Take a moment today to reach out if you need support or remind someone else that it's okay to ask. Let's support each other through the tough times.

We all struggle and suffer; You are not alone in it.

There is no shame in the struggle and suffering;

This is our one common bond.

You are enough; You are loved; You are worthy;

And you will never be alone.

September 16

Checking in on your friends

>>>>>>>

Today, I will make an effort to check in on my friends. I will remind myself that showing up for others creates connection and builds trust.

When was the last time you checked in on your friends? Sometimes, the people who seem the strongest are the ones who need someone to ask how they're doing.

Take a moment today to reach out to a friend. Just let them know you're thinking of them. Let's remind each other to show up for one another.

We all struggle and suffer; You are not alone in it.

There is no shame in the struggle and suffering;

This is our one common bond.

You are enough; You are loved; You are worthy;

And you will never be alone.

September 17

Normalizing emotional conversations

\>>>>>>>

Today, I will remind myself that emotions are part of being human. I will create a safe space for myself and others to share openly and without judgment.

Talking about emotions isn't always easy, especially for men. But here's the truth: it's part of being human, and it's how we connect.

Take a moment today to start a real conversation. Ask how someone's feeling, or share what's on your mind. Let's remind each other that it's okay to feel.

We all struggle and suffer; You are not alone in it.

There is no shame in the struggle and suffering;

This is our one common bond.

You are enough; You are loved; You are worthy;

And you will never be alone.

September 18

Celebrating resilience

>>>>>>>

Today, I will celebrate my resilience and the resilience of those around me. I will remind myself that every challenge faced is a testament to strength.

Resilience isn't about never struggling. It's about how you rise after the fall. And that's something worth celebrating, for yourself and for the people in your life.

Take a moment today to honor your resilience and recognize someone else's. Let's remind each other of our strength.

We all struggle and suffer; You are not alone in it.

There is no shame in the struggle and suffering;

This is our one common bond.

You are enough; You are loved; You are worthy;

And you will never be alone.

September 19

Supporting men in your community

>>>>>>>

Today, I will make an effort to support the men in my community. I will remind myself that lifting others up makes us all stronger.

Supporting other men isn't about fixing their problems. It's about being there, showing up, and letting them know they're not alone.

Take a moment today to offer support, whether it's through listening, sharing advice, or just being present. Let's remind each other that we're in this together.

We all struggle and suffer; You are not alone in it.

There is no shame in the struggle and suffering;

This is our one common bond.

You are enough; You are loved; You are worthy;

And you will never be alone.

September 20

Practicing gratitude for connection

\>>>>>>>

Today, I will be grateful for the connections I have. I will remind myself that relationships are a source of strength and joy in my life.

Sometimes, it's easy to forget how much the people in our lives mean to us. But real, meaningful connection is what keeps us going.

Take a moment today to appreciate the people who've been there for you. Let's remind each other to value our connections.

We all struggle and suffer; You are not alone in it.

There is no shame in the struggle and suffering;

This is our one common bond.

You are enough; You are loved; You are worthy;

And you will never be alone.

# September 21

Encouraging open conversations

\>>>>>>>

Today, I will encourage open conversations with the men in my life. I will remind myself that connection starts with being willing to listen and share.

Have you noticed how rare it is for men to really talk about how they're feeling? But when we have those real, authentic conversations, it can make all the difference.

Take a moment today to ask someone how they're really doing or share something on your mind. Let's remind each other that talking is how we connect.

We all struggle and suffer; You are not alone in it.

There is no shame in the struggle and suffering;

This is our one common bond.

You are enough; You are loved; You are worthy;

And you will never be alone.

September 22

Honoring your emotions

>>>>>>>

Today, I will honor my emotions without judgment. I will remind myself that feeling deeply is a sign of strength, not weakness.

Do you ever feel like you're not supposed to feel certain emotions? Like being upset or overwhelmed somehow makes you less strong? Here's the truth: emotions are human, and honoring them takes strength.

Take a moment today to let yourself feel, but without judgment. Let's remind each other that it's okay to feel.

We all struggle and suffer; You are not alone in it.

There is no shame in the struggle and suffering;

This is our one common bond.

You are enough; You are loved; You are worthy;

And you will never be alone.

September 23

Supporting friends through struggles

>>>>>>>

Today, I will be a source of support for my friends. I will remind myself that showing up for someone in need can change their day and even their life.

Sometimes, being there for a friend is as simple as showing up, listening, or reminding them they're not alone. It might not seem like much, but it can mean everything.

Take a moment today to check in with a friend who might be struggling. Let's remind each other to support one another through the tough times.

We all struggle and suffer; You are not alone in it.

There is no shame in the struggle and suffering;

This is our one common bond.

You are enough; You are loved; You are worthy;

And you will never be alone.

September 24

Letting go of societal expectations

>>>>>>>

Today, I will let go of unrealistic expectations about what it means to be a man. I will remind myself that strength comes from authenticity, not conformity.

There's a lot of pressure to fit into a certain idea of what being a man looks like; always strong, always in control. But here's the thing: real strength comes from being yourself.

Take a moment today to let go of any expectations that don't feel true to who you are. Let's remind each other that authenticity is strength.

We all struggle and suffer; You are not alone in it.

There is no shame in the struggle and suffering;

This is our one common bond.

You are enough; You are loved; You are worthy;

And you will never be alone.

September 25

Finding peace in self-care

>>>>>>>

Today, I will prioritize self-care without guilt. I will remind myself that taking care of myself allows me to show up stronger for others.

Self-care isn't selfish, even though it can feel that way sometimes. Taking care of yourself is how you refill your cup so you can keep giving.

Take a moment today to do one thing that brings you peace or joy. Let's remind each other that self-care is essential.

We all struggle and suffer; You are not alone in it.

There is no shame in the struggle and suffering;

This is our one common bond.

You are enough; You are loved; You are worthy;

And you will never be alone.

September 26

Building a culture of support

>>>>>>>

Today, I will contribute to a culture of support for the men in my life. I will remind myself that we all need someone to lean on.

Men supporting men. It's something we don't talk about enough. But lifting each other up is how we build a stronger, healthier community.

Take a moment today to let a friend know you're there for them, or ask for support if you need it. Let's remind each other that we're in this together.

We all struggle and suffer; You are not alone in it.

There is no shame in the struggle and suffering;

This is our one common bond.

You are enough; You are loved; You are worthy;

And you will never be alone.

September 27

Celebrating progress in mental health

\>>>>>>>

Today, I will celebrate the steps I've taken to prioritize my mental health. I will remind myself that growth is a journey, not a destination.

Mental health is a journey, not something you fix overnight. Every step, big or small, is progress worth celebrating.

Take a moment today to honor one thing you've done for your mental health recently. Let's remind each other that growth takes time.

We all struggle and suffer; You are not alone in it.

There is no shame in the struggle and suffering;

This is our one common bond.

You are enough; You are loved; You are worthy;

And you will never be alone.

September 28

Strengthening trust in relationships

>>>>>>>

Today, I will focus on building trust in my relationships. I will remind myself that trust grows through honesty, effort, and care.

Trust is the foundation of every strong relationship, but it's something you build over time; with honesty, care, and showing up for each other.

Take a moment today to strengthen trust with someone in your life. Let's remind each other that good relationships take effort.

We all struggle and suffer; You are not alone in it.

There is no shame in the struggle and suffering;

This is our one common bond.

You are enough; You are loved; You are worthy;

And you will never be alone.

September 29

Encouraging hope in others

>>>>>>>

Today, I will be a source of hope for those around me. I will remind myself that my words and actions have the power to inspire and uplift others.

Hope can feel hard to find sometimes, but you can be the person who brings it to someone else. A kind word, a reminder of their strength, or just showing you care can go a long way.

Take a moment today to encourage someone, especially a man who might need to hear it. Let's remind each other that hope is contagious.

We all struggle and suffer; You are not alone in it.

There is no shame in the struggle and suffering;

This is our one common bond.

You are enough; You are loved; You are worthy;

And you will never be alone.

September 30

Reflecting on the month's growth

>>>>>>>

Today, I will reflect on how I've grown this month. I will honor the steps I've taken, the challenges I've faced, and the connections I've deepened.

As September comes to an end, take a moment to reflect on this month. Think about the challenges you've faced, the progress you've made, and the people who've supported you along the way.

Celebrate how far you've come, and let it inspire you for the months ahead. Let's remind each other to honor our journeys.

We all struggle and suffer; You are not alone in it.

There is no shame in the struggle and suffering;

This is our one common bond.

You are enough; You are loved; You are worthy;

And you will never be alone.

October 1

Reflecting on your journey

>>>>>>>

Today, I will take time to reflect on my journey so far. I will remind myself that every experience, good or bad, has contributed to my growth.

October is here, and it's the perfect time to pause and reflect. Think about where you started, the progress you've made, and the lessons you've learned along the way.

Take a moment today to honor your journey. Let's remind each other that every step matters, even the hard ones.

We all struggle and suffer; You are not alone in it.

There is no shame in the struggle and suffering;

This is our one common bond.

You are enough; You are loved; You are worthy;

And you will never be alone.

October 2

Practicing gratitude for small moments

>>>>>>>

Today, I will find gratitude in the small moments. I will remind myself that even the simplest joys can brighten my day and lift my spirit.

Gratitude doesn't have to be about big things. Sometimes, it's the small moments; a kind word, a favorite song, the way the sun feels on your face.

Take a moment today to notice and appreciate something simple. Let's remind each other that gratitude changes perspective.

We all struggle and suffer; You are not alone in it.

There is no shame in the struggle and suffering;

This is our one common bond.

You are enough; You are loved; You are worthy;

And you will never be alone.

October 3

Supporting men through difficult times

>>>>>>>

Today, I will make an effort to support the men in my life. I will remind myself that showing up with empathy and care can make a real difference.

Men don't always talk about their struggles, but that doesn't mean they're not there. Sometimes, just letting someone know you're there can make all the difference.

Take a moment today to check in on a man in your life and ask how they're really doing. Let's remind each other that support matters.

We all struggle and suffer; You are not alone in it.

There is no shame in the struggle and suffering;

This is our one common bond.

You are enough; You are loved; You are worthy;

And you will never be alone.

October 4

Honoring your mental health

>>>>>>>

Today, I will honor my mental health by giving myself time and space to process my emotions. I will remind myself that prioritizing my well-being is essential.

Mental health is just as important as physical health, but it's easy to push it to the side, isn't it?

Take a moment today to check in with yourself. How are you feeling, really? Let's remind each other that prioritizing mental health is strength.

We all struggle and suffer; You are not alone in it.

There is no shame in the struggle and suffering;

This is our one common bond.

You are enough; You are loved; You are worthy;

And you will never be alone.

October 5

Letting go of guilt

>>>>>>>

Today, I will let go of the guilt I've been carrying. I will remind myself that I am human, and mistakes are opportunities to grow.

Guilt can feel like a heavy weight, can't it? Like it's holding you back from moving forward. But here's the truth: guilt is just a reminder that you care.

Take a moment today to forgive yourself for one thing and focus on what you've learned. Let's remind each other that we're all a work in progress.

We all struggle and suffer; You are not alone in it.

There is no shame in the struggle and suffering;

This is our one common bond.

You are enough; You are loved; You are worthy;

And you will never be alone.

October 6

Encouraging emotional openness

>>>>>>>

Today, I will remind myself that being emotionally open is a strength. I will create a space for others to share their feelings and be heard without judgment.

Men aren't always encouraged to talk about their emotions, but that doesn't mean they don't need to. Creating space for someone to share can change everything.

Take a moment today to encourage a real, open conversation. Let's remind each other that being open is brave.

We all struggle and suffer; You are not alone in it.

There is no shame in the struggle and suffering;

This is our one common bond.

You are enough; You are loved; You are worthy;

And you will never be alone.

October 7

Finding peace in stillness

>>>>>>>

Today, I will remind myself to slow down and embrace stillness. I will find peace in the quiet moments and let them recharge my mind and spirit.

Life can feel so loud, can't it? Like there's always something demanding your attention. But here's the thing: stillness is where peace lives.

Take a moment today to pause, breathe, and let yourself just be. Let's remind each other that slowing down is a gift.

We all struggle and suffer; You are not alone in it.

There is no shame in the struggle and suffering;

This is our one common bond.

You are enough; You are loved; You are worthy;

And you will never be alone.

October 8

Normalizing self-care for men

>>>>>>>

Today, I will remind myself that self-care is not selfish. It's necessary. I will make time for rest, reflection, and what brings me peace.

Self-care is for everyone, including men. But sometimes it feels like it's not something we're 'supposed' to need, doesn't it?

Take a moment today to prioritize one thing that recharges you; rest, reflection, or something that makes you happy. Let's remind each other that self-care is strength.

We all struggle and suffer; You are not alone in it.

There is no shame in the struggle and suffering;

This is our one common bond.

You are enough; You are loved; You are worthy;

And you will never be alone.

October 9

Finding purpose in helping others

>>>>>>>

Today, I will remind myself that helping others brings purpose to my life. I will support those around me, knowing that small acts of kindness create a ripple effect.

Sometimes, purpose feels like this big, far-off thing, but it can be as simple as helping someone else. A kind word, a small gesture, or just being present can make a huge difference.

Take a moment today to do something kind for someone else. Let's remind each other that purpose grows in connection.

We all struggle and suffer; You are not alone in it.

There is no shame in the struggle and suffering;

This is our one common bond.

You are enough; You are loved; You are worthy;

And you will never be alone.

October 10

Breaking the stigma around men's mental health

>>>>>>>

Today, I will remind myself that mental health is not a weakness. By speaking up and encouraging others to do the same, I help break the stigma.

Men's mental health is so often overlooked or dismissed, isn't it? But here's the truth: talking about it doesn't make you weak, it makes you strong.

Take a moment today to start or encourage a conversation about mental health. Let's remind each other that breaking the stigma starts with us.

We all struggle and suffer; You are not alone in it.

There is no shame in the struggle and suffering;

This is our one common bond.

You are enough; You are loved; You are worthy;

And you will never be alone.

October 11

Supporting yourself through hard times

\>>>>>>>

Today, I will remind myself that it's okay to have hard days. I will show myself compassion and trust that I have the strength to keep going.

Some days feel heavier than others, don't they? It's easy to get frustrated with yourself for struggling, but here's the thing: it's okay to have hard days.

Take a moment today to show yourself the same compassion you'd show a friend. Let's remind each other that we're allowed to struggle and keep moving forward.

We all struggle and suffer; You are not alone in it.

There is no shame in the struggle and suffering;

This is our one common bond.

You are enough; You are loved; You are worthy;

And you will never be alone.

October 12

Finding gratitude in challenges

>>>>>>>

Today, I will find gratitude in the challenges I've faced. I will remind myself that every obstacle has taught me something valuable about myself.

Challenges can feel overwhelming, but they also teach us so much, don't they? About strength, patience, and what we're capable of.

Take a moment today to reflect on something you've learned from a challenge in your life. Let's remind each other that growth often comes through struggle.

We all struggle and suffer; You are not alone in it.

There is no shame in the struggle and suffering;

This is our one common bond.

You are enough; You are loved; You are worthy;

And you will never be alone.

October 13

Checking in with friends

>>>>>>>

Today, I will make an effort to check in with the men in my life. I will remind myself that sometimes, a small act of care can make a big difference.

Do you know someone who might need a check-in? Sometimes, a simple 'How are you really doing?' can mean the world to someone who's struggling.

Take a moment today to reach out to a friend, especially one who might be quiet lately. Let's remind each other that showing up matters.

We all struggle and suffer; You are not alone in it.

There is no shame in the struggle and suffering;

This is our one common bond.

You are enough; You are loved; You are worthy;

And you will never be alone.

October 14

Releasing self-criticism

>>>>>>>

Today, I will let go of self-criticism and embrace self-compassion. I will remind myself that I am doing my best, and that's enough.

Do you ever feel like you're your own worst critic? Like nothing you do is ever good enough? But here's the truth: you're doing your best, and that's enough.

Take a moment today to replace self-criticism with kindness toward yourself. Let's remind each other that self-compassion is strength.

We all struggle and suffer; You are not alone in it.

There is no shame in the struggle and suffering;

This is our one common bond.

You are enough; You are loved; You are worthy;

And you will never be alone.

October 15

Celebrating progress in mental health

\>>>>>>>

Today, I will celebrate the progress I've made in my mental health journey. I will remind myself that growth is worth acknowledging, no matter how small.

Mental health progress isn't always big or obvious. It's in the small steps, the quiet victories. But those steps are worth celebrating.

Take a moment today to honor one thing you've done recently to take care of your mental health. Let's remind each other that every effort matters.

We all struggle and suffer; You are not alone in it.

There is no shame in the struggle and suffering;

This is our one common bond.

You are enough; You are loved; You are worthy;

And you will never be alone.

October 16

Embracing forgiveness

>>>>>>>

Today, I will embrace forgiveness, both for myself and others. I will remind myself that holding onto anger or guilt only holds me back from peace.

Forgiveness isn't about excusing what happened. It's about letting go so you can move forward.

Take a moment today to forgive yourself for something or let go of a grudge you've been carrying. Let's remind each other that forgiveness creates freedom.

We all struggle and suffer; You are not alone in it.

There is no shame in the struggle and suffering;

This is our one common bond.

You are enough; You are loved; You are worthy;

And you will never be alone.

October 17

Normalizing conversations about emotions

>>>>>>>

Today, I will remind myself that talking about emotions is healthy and necessary. I will create space for myself and others to share openly.

Do you ever feel like emotions are something you're supposed to keep to yourself? Like talking about them isn't 'manly'? But here's the truth: sharing emotions is how we heal.

Take a moment today to start a real conversation about how you're feeling or invite someone else to share. Let's remind each other that emotions are part of life.

We all struggle and suffer; You are not alone in it.

There is no shame in the struggle and suffering;

This is our one common bond.

You are enough; You are loved; You are worthy;

And you will never be alone.

October 18

Supporting others with empathy

\>\>\>\>\>\>\>

Today, I will support those around me with empathy. I will remind myself that listening and being present can make a profound difference.

Sometimes, supporting someone isn't about fixing their problems. It's about showing up, listening, and letting them know they're not alone.

Take a moment today to offer empathy to someone who might need it. Let's remind each other that presence is powerful.

We all struggle and suffer; You are not alone in it.

There is no shame in the struggle and suffering;

This is our one common bond.

You are enough; You are loved; You are worthy;

And you will never be alone.

October 19

Celebrating your resilience

\>\>\>\>\>\>\>

Today, I will celebrate my resilience. I will remind myself that every time I've faced a challenge, I've shown strength and courage.

Resilience isn't about never falling. It's about how you rise after every fall. And that's worth celebrating.

Take a moment today to honor your ability to keep going, no matter what life throws at you. Let's remind each other that resilience is a quiet kind of strength.

We all struggle and suffer; You are not alone in it.

There is no shame in the struggle and suffering;

This is our one common bond.

You are enough; You are loved; You are worthy;

And you will never be alone.

October 20

Finding peace in letting go

>>>>>>>

Today, I will let go of what no longer serves me. I will remind myself that releasing the past creates space for growth and new beginnings.

Letting go can feel hard, can't it? Like you're giving up something, even if it's holding you back. But here's the truth: letting go creates space for something better.

Take a moment today to release one thing you've been holding onto; whether it's a regret, a grudge, or a fear. Let's remind each other that peace comes from making room for growth.

We all struggle and suffer; You are not alone in it.

There is no shame in the struggle and suffering;

This is our one common bond.

You are enough; You are loved; You are worthy;

And you will never be alone.

October 21

Embracing your authentic self

>>>>>>>

Today, I will remind myself that being authentic is my greatest strength. I will let go of the need to be someone I'm not and embrace who I truly am.

It's easy to feel like you need to fit into someone else's expectations, isn't it? Like being yourself isn't enough. But here's the truth: your authenticity is your strength.

Take a moment today to show up as yourself, without filters or pretenses. Let's remind each other that being real is what matters most.

We all struggle and suffer; You are not alone in it.

There is no shame in the struggle and suffering;

This is our one common bond.

You are enough; You are loved; You are worthy;

And you will never be alone.

October 22

Supporting mental health awareness

>>>>>>>

Today, I will remind myself that raising awareness about mental health can save lives. I will take a step to support the men in my life and encourage open conversations.

Talking about mental health can feel uncomfortable, but it's one of the most important conversations we can have. For ourselves, and for the men around us.

Take a moment today to start a conversation about mental health. It doesn't have to be super deep. Just share your story or listen to someone else's. Let's remind each other that awareness leads to change.

We all struggle and suffer; You are not alone in it.

There is no shame in the struggle and suffering;

This is our one common bond.

You are enough; You are loved; You are worthy;

And you will never be alone.

October 23

Finding courage in vulnerability

>>>>>>>

Today, I will remind myself that vulnerability is not a weakness. It's a bridge to deeper connections. I will let myself be open and real with others.

Vulnerability can feel risky, can't it? Like showing your true self will push people away. But here's the thing: being open creates connection.

Take a moment today to share something real with someone you trust. Let's remind each other that being vulnerable is brave.

We all struggle and suffer; You are not alone in it.

There is no shame in the struggle and suffering;

This is our one common bond.

You are enough; You are loved; You are worthy;

And you will never be alone.

October 24

Honoring your boundaries

>>>>>>>

Today, I will set and honor my boundaries. I will remind myself that saying no is a way of saying yes to my well-being and peace.

Boundaries can feel hard to set, especially when you worry about letting people down. But here's the truth: boundaries protect your peace.

Take a moment today to set one boundary, even if it's small. Let's remind each other that boundaries are a form of self-respect.

We all struggle and suffer; You are not alone in it.

There is no shame in the struggle and suffering;

This is our one common bond.

You are enough; You are loved; You are worthy;

And you will never be alone.

October 25

Reflecting on lessons learned

>>>>>>>

Today, I will reflect on the lessons I've learned from my challenges. I will remind myself that even the hardest times have taught me something valuable.

Challenges don't always feel like they're teaching us anything in the moment, do they? But when you look back, there's always something to take away.

Take a moment today to reflect on one lesson you've learned from a tough time in your life. Let's remind each other that growth often comes from struggle.

We all struggle and suffer; You are not alone in it.

There is no shame in the struggle and suffering;

This is our one common bond.

You are enough; You are loved; You are worthy;

And you will never be alone.

October 26

Supporting friends in their mental health journeys

>>>>>>>

Today, I will support my friends in their mental health journeys. I will remind myself that being present and listening can make a world of difference.

Sometimes, supporting a friend is as simple as listening. No advice, no fixing, just simply being there.

Take a moment today to check in with a friend and let them know you're there for them. Let's remind each other that showing up matters.

We all struggle and suffer; You are not alone in it.

There is no shame in the struggle and suffering;

This is our one common bond.

You are enough; You are loved; You are worthy;

And you will never be alone.

October 27

Finding gratitude in connection

>>>>>>>

Today, I will be grateful for the connections I have. I will remind myself that relationships bring meaning and strength to my life.

It's easy to take the people in your life for granted, isn't it? To forget how much those connections mean.

Take a moment today to appreciate someone in your life who's been there for you. Let's remind each other that connection is one of life's greatest gifts.

We all struggle and suffer; You are not alone in it.

There is no shame in the struggle and suffering;

This is our one common bond.

You are enough; You are loved; You are worthy;

And you will never be alone.

October 28

Embracing hope for the future

>>>>>>>

Today, I will embrace hope for the future. I will remind myself that no matter how hard things feel now, better days are always ahead.

Hope can feel hard to hold onto when things are tough, or even worse; hope can feel dangerous. But it's important to keep hope alive, even if it's just a small flicker.

Take a moment today to focus on one thing you're looking forward to, no matter how small. Let's remind each other that the future holds possibilities.

We all struggle and suffer; You are not alone in it.

There is no shame in the struggle and suffering;

This is our one common bond.

You are enough; You are loved; You are worthy;

And you will never be alone.

October 29

Finding joy in small victories

\>>>>>>>

Today, I will celebrate the small victories in my life. I will remind myself that every step forward, no matter how small, is worth honoring.

It's easy to overlook the little wins, isn't it? To focus only on the big goals. But every step forward matters.

Take a moment today to celebrate one small thing you've achieved recently. Let's remind each other that progress is always worth celebrating.

We all struggle and suffer; You are not alone in it.

There is no shame in the struggle and suffering;

This is our one common bond.

You are enough; You are loved; You are worthy;

And you will never be alone.

October 30

Building a community of support

>>>>>>>

Today, I will contribute to building a community of support for others. I will remind myself that we are stronger together and that every connection matters.

Building a community starts with small actions; showing up, reaching out, and letting people know they're not alone.

Take a moment today to strengthen one connection in your life, whether it's with a friend, family member, or someone new. Let's remind each other that together, we're stronger.

We all struggle and suffer; You are not alone in it.

There is no shame in the struggle and suffering;

This is our one common bond.

You are enough; You are loved; You are worthy;

And you will never be alone.

October 31

Reflecting on the month's growth

>>>>>>>

Today, I will reflect on how I've grown this month. I will honor the progress I've made, the connections I've strengthened, and the lessons I've learned.

As October comes to a close, take a moment to reflect. Think about the challenges you've faced, the progress you've made, and the people who've supported you along the way.
Celebrate how far you've come, and let it inspire you for the months ahead. Let's remind each other to honor our journeys.

We all struggle and suffer; You are not alone in it.

There is no shame in the struggle and suffering;

This is our one common bond.

You are enough; You are loved; You are worthy;

And you will never be alone.

November 1

Practicing gratitude for new beginnings

>>>>>>>

Today, I will be grateful for the opportunity to start fresh. I will remind myself that every new month is a chance to grow and create something meaningful.

November is here, and it's the perfect time to embrace a fresh start. Each new month is an opportunity to reflect, grow, and create something meaningful in your life.

Take a moment today to set an intention for this month. Big or small. Let's remind each other that every day is a chance to begin again.

We all struggle and suffer; You are not alone in it.

There is no shame in the struggle and suffering;

This is our one common bond.

You are enough; You are loved; You are worthy;

And you will never be alone.

November 2

Supporting men during tough times

>>>>>>>

Today, I will make an effort to support the men in my life. I will remind myself that reaching out can make a difference, even when it feels small.

Do you know a man in your life who might be struggling but isn't saying much about it? Sometimes, all it takes is a message or a simple 'I'm here for you.'

Take a moment today to check in with someone who might need it. Let's remind each other that showing up matters.

We all struggle and suffer; You are not alone in it.

There is no shame in the struggle and suffering;

This is our one common bond.

You are enough; You are loved; You are worthy;

And you will never be alone.

November 3

Practicing generosity

>>>>>>>

Today, I will focus on giving to others, whether it's my time, energy, or kindness. I will remind myself that generosity creates connection and meaning.

Generosity doesn't have to be big to make a difference. A kind word, a helping hand, or simply your time can change someone's day.

Take a moment today to give something to someone. It could be your support, your attention, or your care. Let's remind each other that generosity builds connection.

We all struggle and suffer; You are not alone in it.

There is no shame in the struggle and suffering;

This is our one common bond.

You are enough; You are loved; You are worthy;

And you will never be alone.

November 4

Finding strength in community

>>>>>>>

Today, I will remind myself that I am stronger when I am connected to others. I will make an effort to contribute to the community around me.

Community is where we find strength and belonging, but it takes effort to build and maintain. It starts with showing up for each other.

Take a moment today to connect with your community, whether it's a group of friends, family, or a larger cause. Let's remind each other that we're stronger together.

We all struggle and suffer; You are not alone in it.

There is no shame in the struggle and suffering;

This is our one common bond.

You are enough; You are loved; You are worthy;

And you will never be alone.

November 5

Celebrating your unique impact

>>>>>>>

Today, I will remind myself that my actions, no matter how small, have an impact. I will celebrate the ways I contribute to the lives of others.

Do you ever wonder if what you do really matters? Here's the truth: even the smallest actions have a ripple effect. A kind word, a thoughtful gesture, or just a smile and a nod; they all make a difference.

Take a moment today to celebrate the ways you've positively impacted someone, even if it feels small. Let's remind each other that we all have something to give.

We all struggle and suffer; You are not alone in it.

There is no shame in the struggle and suffering;

This is our one common bond.

You are enough; You are loved; You are worthy;

And you will never be alone.

November 6

Normalizing mental health check-ins

\>\>\>\>\>\>\>

Today, I will normalize talking about mental health. I will remind myself that starting these conversations helps create a culture of support.

Talking about mental health shouldn't feel like a taboo, especially for men. The more we start these conversations, the more we make it normal to ask for and offer help.

Take a moment today to check in with someone or share how you're feeling. Let's remind each other that mental health matters.

We all struggle and suffer; You are not alone in it.

There is no shame in the struggle and suffering;

This is our one common bond.

You are enough; You are loved; You are worthy;

And you will never be alone.

November 7

Being thankful for small joys

>>>>>>>

Today, I will find gratitude in the small joys of life. I will remind myself that happiness is often found in the simplest moments.

Gratitude isn't just for the big things. Sometimes, the smallest joys; a warm drink, a good laugh, or a kind word, are what get us through the day.

Take a moment today to notice and appreciate one small joy in your life. Let's remind each other that gratitude keeps us grounded.

We all struggle and suffer; You are not alone in it.

There is no shame in the struggle and suffering;

This is our one common bond.

You are enough; You are loved; You are worthy;

And you will never be alone.

November 8

Supporting men in their mental health journey

>>>>>>>

Today, I will be a source of support for men navigating mental health challenges. I will remind myself that creating a safe space for them to share can make all the difference.

Men don't always feel comfortable sharing their struggles, but creating a safe space can make it easier. Sometimes, just being there to listen is all it takes.

Take a moment today to be present for someone who might need support. Let's remind each other that no one has to face this alone.

We all struggle and suffer; You are not alone in it.

There is no shame in the struggle and suffering;

This is our one common bond.

You are enough; You are loved; You are worthy;

And you will never be alone.

November 9

Reconnecting with purpose

>>>>>>>

Today, I will take time to reconnect with my purpose. I will remind myself that even small actions contribute to a meaningful life.

Purpose doesn't have to be something big or world-changing. It can be found in the small actions we take every day. Helping a friend, supporting a cause, or simply being present.

Take a moment today to reflect on what gives your life meaning. Let's remind each other that purpose grows from what we care about.

We all struggle and suffer; You are not alone in it.

There is no shame in the struggle and suffering;

This is our one common bond.

You are enough; You are loved; You are worthy;

And you will never be alone.

November 10

Expressing gratitude to others

>>>>>>>

Today, I will express gratitude to those who've supported me. I will remind myself that saying thank you strengthens bonds and shows appreciation.

Gratitude isn't just about what we feel. It's about what we express. Letting someone know they've made a difference in your life can mean so much.

Take a moment today to thank someone who's supported you, whether it's a friend, family member, or mentor. Let's remind each other that gratitude builds connection.

We all struggle and suffer; You are not alone in it.

There is no shame in the struggle and suffering;

This is our one common bond.

You are enough; You are loved; You are worthy;

And you will never be alone.

November 11

Honoring your progress

>>>>>>>

Today, I will honor the progress I've made. I will remind myself that every step forward, no matter how small, is worth celebrating.

Do you ever feel like you're not moving fast enough? Like your progress doesn't count unless it's big? Here's the truth: every small step forward matters.

Take a moment today to honor one thing you've accomplished recently, even if it feels small. Let's remind each other that progress deserves to be celebrated.

We all struggle and suffer; You are not alone in it.

There is no shame in the struggle and suffering;

This is our one common bond.

You are enough; You are loved; You are worthy;

And you will never be alone.

November 12

Supporting others in their struggles

>>>>>>>

Today, I will show up for others who may be struggling. I will remind myself that offering support and a listening ear can bring comfort and strength.

Sometimes, the people around us are carrying things we don't see. A kind word, a listening ear, or just being present can make all the difference.

Take a moment today to check in on someone who might need support. Let's remind each other that showing up matters.

We all struggle and suffer; You are not alone in it.

There is no shame in the struggle and suffering;

This is our one common bond.

You are enough; You are loved; You are worthy;

And you will never be alone.

November 13

Practicing self-compassion

>>>>>>>

Today, I will remind myself that I deserve kindness and patience. I will treat myself with the same compassion I offer to others.

It's easy to be kind to others, but do you offer that same kindness to yourself? Self-compassion isn't selfish. It's how we heal and grow.

Take a moment today to speak kindly to yourself. Let's remind each other that we all deserve compassion, especially from ourselves.

We all struggle and suffer; You are not alone in it.

There is no shame in the struggle and suffering;

This is our one common bond.

You are enough; You are loved; You are worthy;

And you will never be alone.

November 14

Breaking the stigma around men's mental health

>>>>>>>

Today, I will take a step toward breaking the stigma around men's mental health. I will remind myself that talking about struggles shows strength, not weakness.

Men don't always feel comfortable talking about mental health, but starting the conversation can save lives. Strength isn't about hiding struggles. It's about facing them.

Take a moment today to share your story or create a safe space for someone to share theirs. Let's remind each other that breaking the stigma starts with us.

We all struggle and suffer; You are not alone in it.

There is no shame in the struggle and suffering;

This is our one common bond.

You are enough; You are loved; You are worthy;

And you will never be alone.

November 15

Finding joy in helping others

>>>>>>>

Today, I will remind myself that helping others brings joy to my life. I will focus on small ways I can make a positive impact in someone else's day.

Do you know how much joy can come from helping someone else? Even a small gesture; a compliment, a helping hand, or just showing up, can brighten their day and yours.

Take a moment today to do one thing for someone else, no matter how small. Let's remind each other that giving back creates happiness.

We all struggle and suffer; You are not alone in it.

There is no shame in the struggle and suffering;

This is our one common bond.

You are enough; You are loved; You are worthy;

And you will never be alone.

November 16

Releasing comparison

>>>>>>>

Today, I will release the need to compare myself to others. I will remind myself that my journey is unique, and my progress is my own.

Comparison can be such a trap, can't it? It makes you focus on what others have instead of what you've accomplished. But here's the truth: your journey is yours alone.

Take a moment today to focus on your own progress, not someone else's. Let's remind each other that comparison isn't the answer.

We all struggle and suffer; You are not alone in it.

There is no shame in the struggle and suffering;

This is our one common bond.

You are enough; You are loved; You are worthy;

And you will never be alone.

November 17

Gratitude for the people in your life

>>>>>>>

Today, I will express gratitude for the people who have supported and cared for me. I will remind myself that relationships are one of life's greatest gifts.

Who's someone in your life who's made a difference for you? Sometimes, we forget to let those people know how much they mean to us.

Take a moment today to reach out and thank someone who's been there for you. Let's remind each other that expressing gratitude strengthens our connections.

We all struggle and suffer; You are not alone in it.

There is no shame in the struggle and suffering;

This is our one common bond.

You are enough; You are loved; You are worthy;

And you will never be alone.

November 18

Celebrating resilience

>>>>>>>

Today, I will celebrate my resilience. I will remind myself that every challenge I've faced has made me stronger and more capable.

Resilience isn't about never struggling. It's about how you keep going despite the struggles. And that's worth celebrating.

Take a moment today to reflect on how far you've come and the strength it took to get here. Let's remind each other that resilience is something to be proud of.

We all struggle and suffer; You are not alone in it.

There is no shame in the struggle and suffering;

This is our one common bond.

You are enough; You are loved; You are worthy;

And you will never be alone.

November 19

Supporting men's emotional openness

>>>>>>>

Today, I will encourage emotional openness in myself and others. I will remind myself that sharing feelings builds stronger connections and trust.

Talking about emotions isn't always easy, especially for men. But when we open up, it creates a space for connection and trust.

Take a moment today to share how you're feeling with someone you trust, or encourage someone else to do the same. Let's remind each other that being open is how we grow closer.

We all struggle and suffer; You are not alone in it.

There is no shame in the struggle and suffering;

This is our one common bond.

You are enough; You are loved; You are worthy;

And you will never be alone.

November 20

Finding strength in gratitude

>>>>>>>

Today, I will find strength in gratitude. I will remind myself that appreciating the good in my life brings hope and perspective during tough times.

Gratitude has a way of shifting your perspective, doesn't it? Even in hard times, there's always something to be thankful for; a small joy, a kind gesture, or just making it through another day.

Take a moment today to focus on one thing you're grateful for. Let's remind each other that gratitude gives us strength.

We all struggle and suffer; You are not alone in it.

There is no shame in the struggle and suffering;

This is our one common bond.

You are enough; You are loved; You are worthy;

And you will never be alone.

November 21

Honoring your mental health journey

>>>>>>>

Today, I will honor the progress I've made in my mental health journey. I will remind myself that every step, no matter how small, is meaningful.

Taking care of your mental health isn't always easy, is it? But every small step you take matters, whether it's reaching out, taking a break, or asking for help.

Take a moment today to honor the progress you've made, even if it feels small. Let's remind each other that every step forward is worth celebrating.

We all struggle and suffer; You are not alone in it.

There is no shame in the struggle and suffering;

This is our one common bond.

You are enough; You are loved; You are worthy;

And you will never be alone.

November 22

Practicing gratitude for life's lessons

>>>>>>>

Today, I will be grateful for the lessons I've learned, even the hard ones. I will remind myself that growth often comes through challenges.

Life's lessons don't always come easily. But even in the hardest moments, there's something to take away; strength, wisdom, or a new perspective.

Take a moment today to reflect on one lesson you've learned and how it's shaped you. Let's remind each other that growth comes through challenges.

We all struggle and suffer; You are not alone in it.

There is no shame in the struggle and suffering;

This is our one common bond.

You are enough; You are loved; You are worthy;

And you will never be alone.

November 23

Supporting men's mental health awareness

>>>>>>>

Today, I will take a step toward raising awareness for men's mental health. I will remind myself that talking about it helps break the silence and stigma.

Men's mental health is often overlooked, isn't it? But starting the conversation is how we break the stigma and create change.

Take a moment today to share something about mental health or encourage someone else to open up. Let's remind each other that awareness makes a difference.

We all struggle and suffer; You are not alone in it.

There is no shame in the struggle and suffering;

This is our one common bond.

You are enough; You are loved; You are worthy;

And you will never be alone.

November 24

Finding joy in giving back

>>>>>>>

Today, I will find joy in giving back to others. I will remind myself that small acts of kindness create ripples of positivity.

Giving back doesn't have to be big to matter. Sometimes, it's the smallest acts that have the biggest impacts.

Take a moment today to do something kind for someone, no matter how small. Let's remind each other that kindness makes the world brighter.

We all struggle and suffer; You are not alone in it.

There is no shame in the struggle and suffering;

This is our one common bond.

You are enough; You are loved; You are worthy;

And you will never be alone.

November 25

Letting go of self-doubt

>>>>>>>

Today, I will let go of self-doubt and embrace self-confidence. I will remind myself that I am capable, worthy, and ready to face what lies ahead.

Self-doubt can feel so heavy, can't it? It whispers, 'You're not good enough,' or 'You're not ready.' But here's the truth: you are capable.

Take a moment today to replace that doubt with belief in yourself. Let's remind each other that confidence starts within.

We all struggle and suffer; You are not alone in it.

There is no shame in the struggle and suffering;

This is our one common bond.

You are enough; You are loved; You are worthy;

And you will never be alone.

November 26

Expressing gratitude to loved ones

>>>>>>>

Today, I will express gratitude to those who support and care for me. I will remind myself that showing appreciation strengthens relationships.

When was the last time you told someone how much they mean to you? Sometimes, we forget to express gratitude for the people who've been there for us.

Take a moment today to thank someone who's made a difference in your life. Let's remind each other that gratitude strengthens our bonds.

We all struggle and suffer; You are not alone in it.

There is no shame in the struggle and suffering;

This is our one common bond.

You are enough; You are loved; You are worthy;

And you will never be alone.

November 27

Focusing on your strengths

>>>>>>>

Today, I will focus on my strengths. I will remind myself that I have unique abilities and qualities that make me resilient and capable.

It's easy to focus on what we're not good at, isn't it? But what about your strengths? The things that make you resilient, capable, and unique?

Take a moment today to reflect on one of your strengths and how it's helped you. Let's remind each other to honor what makes us strong.

We all struggle and suffer; You are not alone in it.

There is no shame in the struggle and suffering;

This is our one common bond.

You are enough; You are loved; You are worthy;

And you will never be alone.

November 28

Encouraging open conversations

>>>>>>>

Today, I will encourage open and honest conversations with the people around me. I will remind myself that vulnerability creates connection and trust.

Real conversations; ones about emotions, struggles, and hopes build the strongest connections. But starting them can feel really intimidating.

Take a moment today to open up to someone or invite someone else to share. People recognize and respect vulnerability. Let's remind each other that vulnerability is the foundation of building trust.

We all struggle and suffer; You are not alone in it.

There is no shame in the struggle and suffering;

This is our one common bond.

You are enough; You are loved; You are worthy;

And you will never be alone.

November 29

Practicing mindfulness

>>>>>>>

Today, I will practice mindfulness. I will remind myself that staying present helps me find peace and appreciate the moment I'm in.

Life moves fast, doesn't it? It's easy to get caught up in the past or worry about the future and forget about the moment you're living in.

Take a moment today to pause and be present. Notice what's around you, breathe deeply, and just be. Let's remind each other that mindfulness brings peace.

We all struggle and suffer; You are not alone in it.

There is no shame in the struggle and suffering;

This is our one common bond.

You are enough; You are loved; You are worthy;

And you will never be alone.

November 30

Reflecting on gratitude and growth

>>>>>>>

Today, I will reflect on the gratitude I've felt and the growth I've experienced this month. I will remind myself that every moment has shaped who I am.

As November comes to an end, take a moment to reflect. Think about the gratitude you've felt, the challenges you've faced, and the growth you've experienced.

Celebrate how far you've come and look ahead with hope for what's next. Let's remind each other to honor our journeys.

We all struggle and suffer; You are not alone in it.

There is no shame in the struggle and suffering;

This is our one common bond.

You are enough; You are loved; You are worthy;

And you will never be alone.

December 1

Embracing a season of reflection

>>>>>>>

Today, I will take time to reflect on my journey this year. I will remind myself that every step, good or bad, has shaped who I am today.

December is here, and it's the perfect time to reflect on your journey. Think about the challenges you've faced, the progress you've made, and the lessons you've learned.

Take a moment today to honor everything this year has taught you. Let's remind each other that reflection helps us grow.

We all struggle and suffer; You are not alone in it.

There is no shame in the struggle and suffering;

This is our one common bond.

You are enough; You are loved; You are worthy;

And you will never be alone.

December 2

Finding gratitude in the present moment

>>>>>>>

Today, I will focus on the present and find gratitude in where I am right now. I will remind myself that this moment matters.

It's easy to get caught up in the past or worry about the future, isn't it? But the present moment is where life happens.

Take a moment today to notice and appreciate where you are right now. Let's remind each other to find gratitude in the present.

We all struggle and suffer; You are not alone in it.

There is no shame in the struggle and suffering;

This is our one common bond.

You are enough; You are loved; You are worthy;

And you will never be alone.

December 3

Supporting others during the holidays

>>>>>>>

Today, I will make an effort to support those who may feel lonely or overwhelmed during the holidays. I will remind myself that small acts of kindness can mean so much.

The holidays aren't easy for everyone, especially for men who might feel lonely or overwhelmed. A kind word, a check-in, or an invitation can make all the difference.

Take a moment today to reach out to someone who might need it. Let's remind each other that showing up matters.

We all struggle and suffer; You are not alone in it.

There is no shame in the struggle and suffering;

This is our one common bond.

You are enough; You are loved; You are worthy;

And you will never be alone.

December 4

Letting go of holiday stress

\>>>>>>>

Today, I will let go of the stress that can come with the holiday season. I will remind myself to focus on what truly matters; connection and peace.

The holidays can feel overwhelming, can't they? With all the expectations and pressure, it's easy to forget what really matters; connection, peace, and kindness.

Take a moment today to let go of one thing stressing you out and focus on what brings you joy. Let's remind each other that simplicity brings peace.

We all struggle and suffer; You are not alone in it.

There is no shame in the struggle and suffering;

This is our one common bond.

You are enough; You are loved; You are worthy;

And you will never be alone.

December 5

Celebrating progress this year

>>>>>>>

Today, I will celebrate the progress I've made this year. I will remind myself that growth doesn't have to be perfect to be meaningful.

Growth isn't always perfect, and it doesn't have to be. Every step forward, every lesson learned, and every challenge faced is progress.

Take a moment today to reflect on how far you've come this year. Let's remind each other that growth is always worth celebrating.

We all struggle and suffer; You are not alone in it.

There is no shame in the struggle and suffering;

This is our one common bond.

You are enough; You are loved; You are worthy;

And you will never be alone.

December 6

Supporting men's mental health through the holidays

>>>>>>>

Today, I will remind myself that the holidays can be hard for some men. I will make an effort to check in and offer my support.

The holidays can feel isolating for some men, especially if they're carrying things they don't feel comfortable sharing. Sometimes, all it takes is a simple check-in to make a difference.

Take a moment today to ask someone how they're really doing. Let's remind each other that support matters, especially this time of year.

We all struggle and suffer; You are not alone in it.

There is no shame in the struggle and suffering;

This is our one common bond.

You are enough; You are loved; You are worthy;

And you will never be alone.

December 7

Finding joy in small moments

>>>>>>>

Today, I will remind myself to find joy in small moments. I will focus on the little things that bring happiness and light to my day.

Joy doesn't have to come from big, flashy moments. Sometimes, it's in the small things like a favorite song, a quiet evening, or a laugh with a friend.

Take a moment today to notice one small thing that makes you smile. Let's remind each other that joy is all around us.

We all struggle and suffer; You are not alone in it.

There is no shame in the struggle and suffering;

This is our one common bond.

You are enough; You are loved; You are worthy;

And you will never be alone.

December 8

Encouraging open conversations

>>>>>>>

Today, I will create space for open and honest conversations. I will remind myself that vulnerability builds trust and connection.

Talking about emotions isn't always easy, especially for men. But here's the truth: being open creates stronger connections.

Take a moment today to start a real conversation. Whether it's sharing something or asking someone how they're feeling. Let's remind each other that vulnerability brings us closer.

We all struggle and suffer; You are not alone in it.

There is no shame in the struggle and suffering;

This is our one common bond.

You are enough; You are loved; You are worthy;

And you will never be alone.

December 9

Focusing on what truly matters

>>>>>>>

Today, I will focus on what truly matters to me. I will remind myself to let go of distractions and invest my energy in what brings me peace and purpose.

The holidays can come with so many distractions, can't they? It's easy to lose sight of what really matters. Connection, kindness, and peace.

Take a moment today to focus on one thing that truly matters to you. Let's remind each other to prioritize what's important.

We all struggle and suffer; You are not alone in it.

There is no shame in the struggle and suffering;

This is our one common bond.

You are enough; You are loved; You are worthy;

And you will never be alone.

December 10

Being present for others

>>>>>>>

Today, I will be fully present for those around me. I will remind myself that my attention and care are some of the greatest gifts I can offer.

Being present can feel like a challenge in a busy season, but it's one of the best gifts you can give. Your attention, your care; it all matters.

Take a moment today to show up fully for someone, whether it's a friend, family member, or even yourself. Let's remind each other that presence is powerful.

We all struggle and suffer; You are not alone in it.

There is no shame in the struggle and suffering;

This is our one common bond.

You are enough; You are loved; You are worthy;

And you will never be alone.

December 11

Supporting others with kindness

>>>>>>>

Today, I will show kindness to others, especially those who might be struggling this season. I will remind myself that small acts of care can have a big impact.

Kindness doesn't have to be grand. It can be as simple as a smile, a thoughtful text, or just listening to someone. Especially during this time of year, those small actions matter.

Take a moment today to show kindness to someone around you. Let's remind each other that little things make a big difference.

We all struggle and suffer; You are not alone in it.

There is no shame in the struggle and suffering;

This is our one common bond.

You are enough; You are loved; You are worthy;

And you will never be alone.

December 12

Letting go of perfection during the holidays

>>>>>>>

Today, I will remind myself that the holidays don't have to be perfect to be meaningful. I will focus on what brings joy, not stress.

The holidays can come with so much pressure, can't they? To make everything perfect, to meet every expectation. But here's the truth: what matters is the joy, not perfection.

Take a moment today to let go of one expectation that's causing you stress. Let's remind each other to focus on what truly matters.

We all struggle and suffer; You are not alone in it.

There is no shame in the struggle and suffering;

This is our one common bond.

You are enough; You are loved; You are worthy;

And you will never be alone.

December 13

Celebrating the people who've supported you

>>>>>>>

Today, I will celebrate the people who've been there for me this year. I will remind myself that gratitude strengthens the bonds we share.

Who's someone who's been there for you this year? It's easy to forget to let those people know how much they mean to us.

Take a moment today to thank someone who's supported you, whether it's a friend, family member, or mentor. Let's remind each other that gratitude keeps relationships strong.

We all struggle and suffer; You are not alone in it.

There is no shame in the struggle and suffering;

This is our one common bond.

You are enough; You are loved; You are worthy;

And you will never be alone.

December 14

Reflecting on your growth

>>>>>>>

Today, I will reflect on the growth I've experienced this year. I will remind myself that every challenge has shaped me into who I am today.

This time of year is the perfect time for reflection. Think about how much you've grown; the lessons you've learned, the challenges you've overcome, and the strength you've gained.

Take a moment today to honor your growth. Let's remind each other that every experience shapes us for the better.

We all struggle and suffer; You are not alone in it.

There is no shame in the struggle and suffering;

This is our one common bond.

You are enough; You are loved; You are worthy;

And you will never be alone.

December 15

Encouraging men to open up

>>>>>>>

Today, I will encourage the men in my life to open up about how they're feeling. I will remind myself that creating space for honesty can change lives.

Men often feel like they can't talk about how they're really feeling, but those conversations can be life-changing.

Take a moment today to check in on a man in your life. Ask how they're doing, and really listen. Let's remind each other that opening up takes strength.

We all struggle and suffer; You are not alone in it.

There is no shame in the struggle and suffering;

This is our one common bond.

You are enough; You are loved; You are worthy;

And you will never be alone.

December 16

Finding peace in stillness

>>>>>>>

Today, I will slow down and find peace in stillness. I will remind myself that rest is essential for renewal and growth.

With all the busyness of the season, it's easy to forget to take a moment for yourself, isn't it? But stillness is where peace lives.

Take a moment today to slow down, breathe, and just be. Let's remind each other that rest is not a luxury. It's necessary.

We all struggle and suffer; You are not alone in it.

There is no shame in the struggle and suffering;

This is our one common bond.

You are enough; You are loved; You are worthy;

And you will never be alone.

December 17

Giving back to others

>>>>>>>

Today, I will focus on giving back to others. I will remind myself that generosity, in any form, creates connection and purpose.

Giving back doesn't have to be about money or big gestures. Sometimes, it's your time, your care, or a small act of kindness that makes the biggest impact.

Take a moment today to give back in a way that feels meaningful to you. Let's remind each other that generosity brings us closer.

We all struggle and suffer; You are not alone in it.

There is no shame in the struggle and suffering;

This is our one common bond.

You are enough; You are loved; You are worthy;

And you will never be alone.

December 18

Practicing gratitude for simple joys

>>>>>>>

Today, I will find gratitude in life's simple joys. I will remind myself that happiness often comes from the little things.

Joy doesn't have to come from grand moments. It's often in the small, everyday things: a good meal, a warm conversation, or even just a quiet moment.

Take a moment today to notice and appreciate one simple joy. Let's remind each other that gratitude starts with the little things.

We all struggle and suffer; You are not alone in it.

There is no shame in the struggle and suffering;

This is our one common bond.

You are enough; You are loved; You are worthy;

And you will never be alone.

December 19

Focusing on connection

\>>>>>>>

Today, I will prioritize connection. I will remind myself that relationships bring meaning and strength to my life.

With everything going on, it's easy to feel disconnected, isn't it? But connection; real, meaningful connection, is what gives life purpose.

Take a moment today to reach out to someone you care about, even if it's just to say hello. Let's remind each other that connection is what keeps us going.

We all struggle and suffer; You are not alone in it.

There is no shame in the struggle and suffering;

This is our one common bond.

You are enough; You are loved; You are worthy;

And you will never be alone.

December 20

Preparing for renewal

\>>>>>>>

Today, I will remind myself that the end of the year is a time for renewal. I will let go of what no longer serves me and make space for new beginnings.

As the year winds down, it's the perfect time to let go of what's been holding you back. Whether it's a habit, a thought, or a regret, releasing it creates space for something new.

Take a moment today to think about one thing you're ready to leave behind. Let's remind each other that renewal begins with letting go.

We all struggle and suffer; You are not alone in it.

There is no shame in the struggle and suffering;

This is our one common bond.

You are enough; You are loved; You are worthy;

And you will never be alone.

December 21

Embracing the season of giving

>>>>>>>

Today, I will embrace the season of giving. I will remind myself that generosity, no matter how small, brings light to those around me.

The holidays are often called the season of giving, but giving doesn't have to be material. It can be your time, your care, or your support.

Take a moment today to offer something to someone else; a kind gesture, a thoughtful word, or a helping hand. Let's remind each other that generosity creates connection.

We all struggle and suffer; You are not alone in it.

There is no shame in the struggle and suffering;

This is our one common bond.

You are enough; You are loved; You are worthy;

And you will never be alone.

December 22

Finding strength in vulnerability

>>>>>>>

Today, I will remind myself that vulnerability is a form of courage. I will allow myself to be open and honest, knowing that it strengthens my relationships.

Being vulnerable isn't easy, is it? It can feel like you're exposing too much. But here's the truth: vulnerability is what builds trust and connection.

Take a moment today to share something real with someone you trust. Let's remind each other that being open is brave.

We all struggle and suffer; You are not alone in it.

There is no shame in the struggle and suffering;

This is our one common bond.

You are enough; You are loved; You are worthy;

And you will never be alone.

December 23

Focusing on what truly matters

>>>>>>>

Today, I will focus on what truly matters this holiday season. I will remind myself that connection and kindness are more important than perfection.

It's easy to get caught up in the hustle and expectations of the holidays, isn't it? But what truly matters is the people you care about and the kindness you share.

Take a moment today to let go of one holiday stress and focus on what brings you joy. Let's remind each other that simplicity often brings the most peace.

We all struggle and suffer; You are not alone in it.

There is no shame in the struggle and suffering;

This is our one common bond.

You are enough; You are loved; You are worthy;

And you will never be alone.

December 24

Supporting those who feel alone during the holidays

>>>>>>>

Today, I will reach out to those who might feel alone during the holidays. I will remind myself that my care and presence can make someone feel seen and valued.

The holidays aren't easy for everyone, especially for those who feel alone. Sometimes, a simple check-in or kind gesture can make all the difference.

Take a moment today to reach out to someone who might need support. Let's remind each other that no one has to face this season alone.

We all struggle and suffer; You are not alone in it.

There is no shame in the struggle and suffering;

This is our one common bond.

You are enough; You are loved; You are worthy;

And you will never be alone.

December 25

Finding gratitude in togetherness

>>>>>>>

Today, I will find gratitude in the people around me. I will remind myself that togetherness, even in small moments, is a gift.

Whether your holidays are full of family and friends or quieter this year, togetherness can mean so many things. It's about connection, care, and gratitude for those around you.

Take a moment today to appreciate the people in your life who make it brighter. Let's remind each other that connection is the heart of this season.

We all struggle and suffer; You are not alone in it.

There is no shame in the struggle and suffering;

This is our one common bond.

You are enough; You are loved; You are worthy;

And you will never be alone.

December 26

Reflecting on the year's lessons

>>>>>>>

Today, I will reflect on the lessons this year has taught me. I will remind myself that every experience, good or bad, has helped me grow.

The end of the year is a time to look back. What challenges have you faced? What lessons have you learned? Every experience, even the tough ones, has shaped who you are.

Take a moment today to reflect on one lesson from this year and how it's helped you grow. Let's remind each other that growth comes through reflection.

We all struggle and suffer; You are not alone in it.

There is no shame in the struggle and suffering;

This is our one common bond.

You are enough; You are loved; You are worthy;

And you will never be alone.

December 27

Letting go of regrets

>>>>>>>

Today, I will let go of regrets and focus on the present. I will remind myself that the past cannot be changed, but the future is mine to create.

Regrets can feel heavy, can't they? But carrying them doesn't change the past, it only holds you back from the future.

Take a moment today to release one regret and focus on what's ahead. Let's remind each other that letting go creates space for new beginnings.

We all struggle and suffer; You are not alone in it.

There is no shame in the struggle and suffering;

This is our one common bond.

You are enough; You are loved; You are worthy;

And you will never be alone.

December 28

Celebrating resilience

>>>>>>>

Today, I will celebrate my resilience. I will remind myself that every challenge I've faced has made me stronger and more capable.

This year has likely had its fair share of challenges, hasn't it? But every time you got back up, you showed resilience.
Take a moment today to honor your strength and the ways you've grown this year. Let's remind each other that resilience is something to be proud of.

We all struggle and suffer; You are not alone in it.

There is no shame in the struggle and suffering;

This is our one common bond.

You are enough; You are loved; You are worthy;

And you will never be alone.

December 29

Setting intentions for the new year

>>>>>>>

Today, I will set intentions for the year ahead. I will remind myself that small, meaningful steps can lead to big changes.

The end of the year isn't just about reflection. It's about looking forward, too. What do you want to focus on in the year ahead? Take a moment today to set one small intention for the new year. Let's remind each other that meaningful change starts with small steps.

We all struggle and suffer; You are not alone in it.

There is no shame in the struggle and suffering;

This is our one common bond.

You are enough; You are loved; You are worthy;

And you will never be alone.

December 30

Expressing gratitude for this year

>>>>>>>

Today, I will express gratitude for the experiences and people who've shaped my year. I will remind myself that every moment has value.

This year might not have been perfect, but it's given you lessons, moments of joy, and people who've supported you.
Take a moment today to express gratitude for one thing that's made this year meaningful. Let's remind each other to honor the journey.

We all struggle and suffer; You are not alone in it.

There is no shame in the struggle and suffering;

This is our one common bond.

You are enough; You are loved; You are worthy;

And you will never be alone.

December 31

Embracing hope for the new year

>>>>>>>

Today, I will embrace hope for the year ahead. I will remind myself that every ending is a new beginning, full of potential and possibility.

As this year ends, it's time to look forward with hope. The new year is a fresh start, a chance to grow, and an opportunity to create something meaningful.
Take a moment today to embrace hope for what's to come. Let's remind each other that the best is yet to come.

We all struggle and suffer; You are not alone in it.

There is no shame in the struggle and suffering;

This is our one common bond.

You are enough; You are loved; You are worthy;

And you will never be alone.

www.ingramcontent.com/pod-product-compliance
Lightning Source LLC
LaVergne TN
LVHW020925090426
835512LV00020B/3203